# Clearing

# Clearing

*A Guide to Liberating Energies*
*Trapped in Buildings and Lands*

Jim PathFinder Ewing

FINDHORN PRESS

Findhorn Press
One Park Street
Rochester, Vermont 05767
www.findhornpress.com

Findhorn Press is a division of Inner Traditions International

ISBN 978-1-84409-082-2

Cataloging-in-Publication Data for this title is available from the British Library


Printed and bound in the United States

Edited by Ellen Kleiner, Blessingway Authors' Services,
134 East Lupita Road, Santa Fe, NM 87505
Cover design by Damian Keenan
Text design by Pam Bochel
Proofread by Kate Keogan
Illustrations by Annette Waya Ewing

*To Quan Yin, Rainbow Woman,*
*Earth Mother, Mother Mary,*
*and all other goddesses of flesh and spirit.*

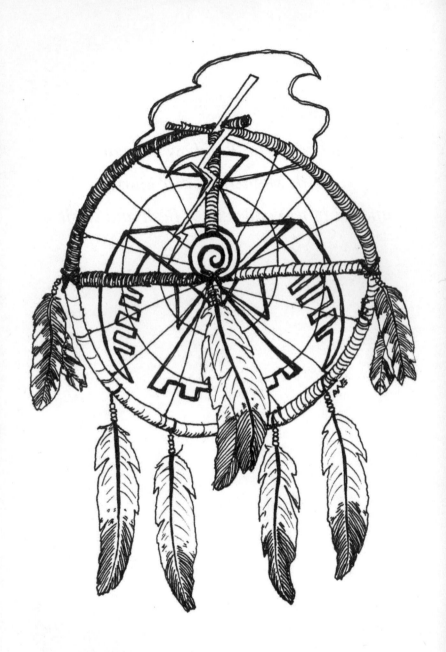

# Contents

Foreword                                                          i
Getting Started                                                   v

**Chapter One: Identifying Places of Sadness,
Suffering, or Agitation**                                        1
    Finding the Stillpoint                    2
    Grounding, Centering, and Shielding       5
    Becoming Proficient at "Reading" Places   6
    From the Energy Notebook: An Instructive
        Gift from Guides  9
    Review                                   10

**Chapter Two: Preparing to Liberate Trapped
Energies**                                                       12
    Ley Lines, Sacred Sites, and the Christ
        Consciousness Grid  16
    Water Sources and Embedded Energy         18
    Burial Spots                              19
    Ghosts and Unwanted Entities              20
    Other Beings                              22
    Portals                                   25
    Guides, Angels, Goddesses, and Power
        Animals           26
    From the Energy Notebook: The Power
        of Dreaming       34
    Review                                   37

**Chapter Three: Meeting the Spirits of the Land**   39
    Perceiving Divine Energies                43
    Finding Wild Spirits, or Allies           44

Discovering Power Animals 48
Recognizing Goddesses and Other Local
    Deities 50
Requesting Assistance from Divine Beings
    and Power Animals 55
From the Energy Notebook: Following a
    "Niggling" Feeling 60
From the Energy Notebook: Drumming
    Up the Sun 62
Review 63

**Chapter Four: Performing Release Ceremonies** 64
Indoor Spaces 64
Large Buildings 70
Outdoor Spaces 74
Liberating Slumbering Earth Energies 78
From the Energy Notebook: A Complex
    Cleansing 81
Review 84

Final Thoughts 86
Other Resources 88
Notes 89
Glossary 96
Bibliography 103

# Foreword

Jim is a voice for the Earth, giving us much needed inspiration and information about living in harmony. And he is, as I consider myself to be, a practical teacher in the realm of Spirit. In this book, he helps us bridge the gap between the energetic realm—a realm more subtle than that which our culture has taught us to perceive, let alone be able to manipulate or transmute—and the world of matter and solid objects with which we are more familiar and comfortable. Although I consider this book a marvelous guide in its specific focus of identifying and transmuting energies in order to live in greater harmony with our environment, I also sense that it is of broader import than that: it provides an effective metaphorical bridge for us as we walk toward working with the energetic realm in all aspects of our lives.

As we approach the prophesied Golden time of harmony, beauty, and peace becoming realized on this sweet Earth, it is clear that our most powerful and useful interaction with the world around us can often be an energetic one. Won't it be wonderful when we create a dream / plan, focus our love and attention on it, and the larger world conspires with us to bring something into manifestation? How different from  our present, energetically-draining practice of pushing and shoving around the weighty material world! Will it not be magnificent when we move into the non-manifest realm and do our gentle work there, rather than use the personal power it takes to attempt to make major changes from the material plane? To make this more concrete, I offer you an example from the healing work which many of us experience. On a weekly basis we can massage the kinks and tensions out of a fast-paced executive's body whose mind-set is that of a worrier. Or, more effectively in terms of energy and time, we can move into his light body and change any choices/patterns involving strain, worry, fearfulness and over-work. We go into the energetic body, to the pattern in the etheric realm where the person's patterns are set, and there shift the pattern, so that all future manifestations through that particular window are forever changed. This means that not only is it easier to make the changes, but also that the new pattern holds over time; it's not just a one-shot deal, but lives on out into his life. The executive (or any one of us) walks forward with more ease and confidence, as well as openness to input and perception, thus making the completion of tasks more efficient and easeful, perhaps even joyful. He even has more personal energy left to do the specific work needed on the material level, and perhaps even a bit more for his family when he gets home, too.

This way of working within ourselves and with the world around us is the most useful thing we can be learning at this point in time. Jim gives us simple and clear ways to make this energetic connection, understanding that opening to wisdom from the realm of guides and spirits anchors us in that higher focus and allows us to receive the information we need to make a difference in the specific situation we face.

Becoming aware of situations and places in which the energy is less than positive, less than harmonious, is a first and very powerful step. We become aware and stand in a place of power to make positive changes. These changes harmonize not only the specific situation or place concerned, but add a sweeter energy to the whole Earth. In becoming more aware, we become more perceptive, more sensitive, more present in the rich, sweet world of this amazing planet, our Lady Gaia. And perhaps more willing to honor and respect all that we see and feel. As each of us uses our consciousness and intent to make these changes, the world continues to grow in beauty, peace, and harmony. We do our part to bring about the Golden time; it is right and good that we do so.

Brooke Medicine Eagle
Sky Lodge, Montana
April 2006

*The land and rocks speak, if only we listen.*

*Their spirits give visions, if only we see.*

*Their voices bestow wisdom when we are silent
enough to hear.*

*With the Creator, we can create miracles.*

*Wouldn't life be grand if every space were fit
for a goddess?*

# Getting Started

Have you ever walked into a room and felt a chill, or that something wasn't quite right? Or have you entered a space and suddenly become sad or agitated for no apparent reason? On the other hand, are there places which you have visited that consistently bring about an inexplicable sense of contentment?

All the spaces we inhabit—the places where we live, work, or visit for various reasons—may harbor spirits or types of energy that affect our well-being. If spirits are trapped, their energies may cause us mental or emotional distress, while in other cases their presence can uplift us emotionally or contribute to a wholesome state of mind. Additionally, energy patterns in structures or on land can be either negative or positive, depending on their origin and vibrational rate. Fortunately, spaces can be cleared by liberating trapped spirits and then transmuting any negative energy to positive energy by raising its vibrational rate. Given proper instruction, anyone can do this without expert intervention—with the assistance of guides and spirit helpers, instead, who actually do the work—despite the fact that in our materialistic society, there is a bias against believing in the reality of anything that can't be touched or measured.

Everyone has the capacity to perceive phenomena energetically and to work with energy. This capacity only needs to be developed, just as you would have to tune a radio in to the waves being continually broadcast. Once the proper techniques are mastered, it is possible to sense the energy of spaces and coordinate activities to effectively discern and work with energy for greater health and harmony.

As a practitioner of "environmental shamanism," affecting the essential nature of places, I am often asked to clear spaces—that is, to dissipate or transmute negative energy—when people move to a new house or apartment. Likewise, I am routinely requested to cleanse business locations, transmuting energy to a more positive form by raising the vibrational rate, and thus making the space more attractive to employees and customers so that business improves. A frequent comment after such spaces have been cleared or cleansed is, "I can't believe how delightful this place feels!" The effects from even one treatment can last for months, prompting visitors entering after a long absence to feel like a light has been turned on. Similarly, when tracts of land are cleared or cleansed, the changes can be just as evident—as in a flourishing of flora and fauna, for example. Such transformations in the energy of structures or landscapes often increase abundance, catalyze healing, or inspire human creativity.

Nearly any space can be improved energetically as long as its composition and properties are comprehended. Fundamental to such an understanding is basic knowledge of physics: just as a house or other structure has enclosed space, objects that appear solid (such as rocks) contain more space between the atoms, nuclei, electrons, protons, and quarks than matter—

roughly equivalent, proportionally, to the spaces between the sun and planets in the solar system. Further, all this space between matter (in addition to the space around us that contains matter) is capable of holding positive or negative vibrations of energy. Vibrational frequency in the spaces between matter is what characterizes all energy, whether its effects on people are positive or negative. When a person enters a room and feels "chill bumps" for no apparent reason or gravitates toward a spot that inspires joy, these reactions are based on subtle internal sensibilities in response to vibrational frequencies within the spaces.

The purpose of this book is to help readers live in harmony with the buildings and lands they love by learning how to identify and transmute various kinds of energies, changing them from one form to another. Although most people may be unaccustomed to transmuting energies per se, they are familiar with transmuting water and matter. Water can easily be transmuted by altering its temperature: when frozen, it is ice; when heated, it becomes vapor; when cooled, it condenses back into water. Matter can be transmuted by burning it or leaving it out in the elements to decay. Likewise, it is possible to transmute energies—cause their patterns to change—through intent, by developing the practices and performing the ceremonies taught in this book. People sometimes ask, "How do you do this work, this transmuting and healing of spaces?" The answer is really quite simple: I don't do it; the guides and spirit helpers do it. A great truth too rarely understood is that humans are the only physical beings on the planet who have self-consciousness and thus walk between the worlds of substance and spirit; when we realize our potential power and are guided by spirit we are capable of much beneficial energy work for the common good of the planet.

The book focuses on basic instruction, including exercises to develop capabilities for working with energy, as well as suggestions for discerning when assistance is required and how to seek it from guides and spirit helpers. Readers are encouraged to keep a notebook of observations that might prove useful in future clearings; some entries from my own notebook are provided as samples. Each chapter concludes with an at-a-glance review of major points for easy reference.

A portion of the sale of each book will be donated to nonprofit organizations dedicated to acquiring and preserving Native American sacred sites so that all may benefit from this gift of the Creator.

# Chapter One

# Identifying Places of Sadness, Suffering, or Agitation

*Know thyself.*

INSCRIPTION AT THE DELPHIC ORACLE

Most places that need clearing broadcast the fact strongly by exuding negative energy, causing a distinctly oppressive feeling, but it takes practice to "read" and interpret types of energy. The key to identifying places which need clearing of sadness, suffering, or agitation is knowing your personal energy and becoming more sensitive to the energy around you. It is necessary to perceive the subtle vibrations of both external and internal energy patterns; this is a capability that usually has to be learned. Since people generally tend to be more extroverted than introverted, and since our culture does not encourage discernment between types of energy in daily life (through ritual, for example, as did many ancient cultures) such perception takes practice. Intuitively, we are all aware of the power of personal energy. Upon entering a room, we have all unexpectedly experienced strong feelings emanating from someone— a rival in business, a former lover, or even a stranger. We also know from movies of the "one look across a crowded room." The intuitive faculty picks up the energy of another and translates it into feelings.

Although we are often aware of sensing the energy of people and places, rarely are we taught how to perceive energetic qualities consciously or how to use them advantageously. Gaining the ability to consciously perceive and beneficially transmute energy patterns takes training, like learning to read and write. Initially, squiggly lines in books are unintelligible to a child, who later is able to understand their meaning. Similarly, it is possible to learn how to "read" the interior spaces of structures and the exterior spaces of land if we first learn the "alphabet" of their energy patterns by becoming aware of subtleties within our own inner spaces and accessing our intuition. We do this by finding our Stillpoint, the place in our being of total silence and stillness.

## Finding the Stillpoint

The ability to discover the Stillpoint is a prerequisite for learning to "read" energy and transmute it for increased health. The Stillpoint is where intuition and creativity originate, and where balance is achieved through relaxation and centering. It is the source of being, where individuals exist as their most authentic selves. The Stillpoint is a key element in spiritual practice, inviting recognition of the sacred in all things through awareness of the sacred in oneself. The Stillpoint may be accessed in any number of ways, and all techniques for discovering it lead to two empowering realizations: the world is a rich place that can inspire infinite exploration, and you can access your Stillpoint whenever you choose because stillness is within and not something to be sought outside yourself.

One method of discovering the Stillpoint is simply to do something that you love—such as painting, writing, knitting, playing a musical instrument, or making model airplanes—allowing total absorption in the activity to lead you to inner stillness. Alternatively, the Stillpoint can be found more deliberately by becoming increasingly aware of living in the present moment, with no thought about what you did yesterday or plan to do tomorrow, thus stopping accustomed mind chatter. A third means of locating the Stillpoint is through meditation. When doing a meditation practice, keep in mind that it is most likely to lead to the Stillpoint and remain sacred if there is a beginning, middle, and end.

The following is one such meditation practice: Place your hands in the prayer position and focus on your middle fingers. As thoughts arise, consciously dismiss them without anger or annoyance, with patience and gentleness toward yourself, understanding that the proliferation of thoughts is a deeply entrenched habit of the ego in order to sustain its existence. With practice, you can succeed in breaking this habit of involuntary mental activity, achieving refreshing clarity.[1]

Another meditation concerns being fully present with whatever you perceive. For example, hold an egg in your hand and study it, taking in as much information as possible: its weight, shape, texture. To deepen your awareness of the egg, recognize and then release any prior associations you may have with it— such as a childhood memory of an Easter egg hunt or of cooking omelets with a loved one. Whatever thoughts or memories surface, acknowledge them, experience them, and then let them go. As they are released, you may feel more relaxed and gain a deeper awareness of both the essence of the egg and your unique consciousness.

Finally, the most fundamental meditation is to become aware of how breathing affects energy flow and states of consciousness. Breathe deeply from the pelvic region, pushing your belly out and expanding your lungs until they feel full, then hold your breath briefly before exhaling gently, contracting your belly until your lungs feel empty. Settling into a gentle rhythm, with each inhalation feel energy coming in and envision your consciousness expanding; with each exhalation feel tensions in your body being released. In this state of simply breathing and being, explore your surroundings with your mind, heart, and full range of senses. What is the quietest sound you can hear? Is it internal or external? What does the silence "taste" like? What do you "see" without looking? How much can you perceive through the simple act of breathing? Where inside you have you gained awareness through experiencing life without an agenda?

Accessing the Stillpoint enhances both your perception and your ability to envision potential and be creative. Once your Stillpoint is found, learn to operate from that space confidently and fearlessly. Then you will be able to affect the energy of a place as you choose, from a centered state of "knowing" that is neutral, protected, and empowered. This is done by grounding, centering, and shielding.

## Grounding, Centering, and Shielding

Grounding entails connecting energetically with the earth to ensure that consciousness is not operating from other dimensions or overly-affected by other energetic forces. To ground yourself, visualize a thread of energy extending from the base of the spine (the pelvic floor or perineum, the root chakra) deep into the earth, imagining that it connects you to the healing and life-sustaining power of the earth and provides support wherever you go. Do this at intervals throughout the day to reaffirm your established connection, preferably leaning against a rock or tree—something that touches the root chakra and enables you to feel linked to the physicality of the earth in order to minimize influence from the energy forces of other dimensions.

Centering involves locating the core of consciousness in the body and drawing earth energy from below and higher perception from above in order to operate from a balanced awareness. To center yourself, feel the earth's energy, the life-giving power of nature, coming up through your feet and legs into your midsection. Simultaneously, sense the life-giving energy of the sun—or of the stars at night—flowing through the top of your head (the crown chakra) and into your midsection, where it meets the earth energy coming up from below.

Using this process to create a "knowing space" will protect you from upsets and allow you to function in a balanced manner.

Shielding is to create, through intent, a protective energy layer around yourself in order to deflect external negative energy. To shield yourself, visualize a cocoon of mirrors surrounding you, reflecting unwanted energy outwards. Put this invisible armor on as you would a coat. You can envision it as simply a bubble of white or blue light; it is a shield, but not a veil, to protect you, not to remove you from anything. Merely knowing that this shield is keeping you safe and that you can summon it to envelop you simply through intention will deflect all negative energy. From time to time, energize the protective quality of the shield by re-affirming your intention.

## Becoming Proficient at "Reading" Places

People are always relating with their environments on an unconscious level, and learning to "read" the qualities and types of energy in various locations can be advantageous for balanced living. To become proficient at "reading" places, start by noticing energy around you wherever you go. If you suddenly find yourself distracted, sad, or irritated, try to see or feel the energy of the place and determine what may have caused the emotion. As you are assessing locations and types of energy, clear your mind of preconceived assumptions and judgments about the place or objects in it; such conditioned responses are the principal obstacles to assessing energy accurately. Awaken inner faculties that have been dormant in order to see or feel the ebb and flow of energy.

In addition to practicing assessing qualities and types of energy in various locations, you can also hone your senses (see Exercise 1) and increase your knowledge of the potential significance of energies. For example, if a strong energy emanates from a particular object which seems symbolic, research where it came from and what cultures use such objects, as well as the qualities associated with it, and then record your discoveries in a notebook for future reference. In this way your observations will lead to a continuing education that both sharpens your senses and broadens your general knowledge. At times these observations may unexpectedly result in important revelations for self-knowledge and personal development.

### Exercise 1: Accentuating the Senses through the Power of Opposites

Senses may be heightened in order to enable better "reading" of energy in spaces by utilizing the power of opposites. For example, if a warm object is held in the hand and then something cold is touched, the sensation of coldness will be accentuated. The same principle may be applied to the experiencing of energies attached to a particular area. To increase your awareness of this potential, go to a place where intense feelings of both sadness and joy have transpired and compare their energies. Begin by accessing your Stillpoint; then ground, center, and shield. Approach this space as a neutral observer, trying to feel all the types of existent energy. In this way, you will gain maximum awareness of the site's energies. Make a game of it: imagine yourself guiding someone who is blind, while observing and reporting everything that might prove valuable to that individual. Carry a notebook and jot down your impressions. The intention is not to be affected by the energies but rather to identify their subtleties.

Softening your focus, either through gazing from the side or squinting, feel the energies and try to sense the source from which they are emanating. Then, closing your eyes, notice if you become conscious of an emotion and what may be triggering it. If you are outdoors, are the energies affected by the arrangement of the natural or urban landscape? By how the houses or other structures are situated? By how features of the terrain are geometrically related to one another? If you are indoors, are the energies affected by the arrangement of rooms or interior objects? What precisely are the energized elements, and what is the nature of that energy? After practicing this exercise, it may become evident that sensory awareness is accentuated by the simultaneous existence of opposite types of energy.

In order to practice a variation on this exercise, go to a place which has energies which you wish to change and follow the same steps. See if certain features or objects exude different types of energy; assess what kinds of energy they emit, and consider how they affect you. Then decide how you wish to shift this energy. Although it will take continued practice to discern the "alphabet" of energy and to become adept at "reading" it, this exercise can make you more aware of opposing energy forces, as well as of the full spectrum of energies affecting various locations.

## *From the Energy Notebook:*
## *An Instructive Gift from Guides*

A few years ago, researching the origin of an object and the qualities associated with it led to a significant revelation for my personal development. Someone presented me with a curious gift—an ugly, rusty, animal trap—after finding it in a tumbled-down shack by a river and following the advice of his guides, who told him that it would present me with a valuable lesson. It is always important to trust guides, since as powers of the universe they have more information than we do, so I accepted the unusual gift as the positive offering it was intended to be. However, realizing that a person's preconceived assumptions and judgments are the principal obstacles to assessing the energy of an object or place, I had to overcome my prejudices about trapping animals and view the object with detachment.

For weeks the trap sat in a corner as it became increasingly obvious that the gift held some kind of strange power. This was reflected in the reactions of various people, who would glance toward the trap even though it was almost hidden from view, while their faces darkened momentarily. Eventually, it became apparent that the trap was actually collecting negative energy. The original owner had cared for the trap as a precious tool of his livelihood and although he was no longer alive, the power of his intent and the resultant pattern of energy remained embedded in the object. The trap was still functioning as intended, but in accordance with its new surroundings—instead of trapping animals it was trapping negative energy, which was the intended "prey" of its new owner. The trap actually adapted to my own intent and energetic environment. That is, I saw that the guides of the gift-giver had indeed shared with me a great lesson: how we treat objects affects their essential energy since our intent can become embedded in their energy. Once I learned this lesson, I placed the trap on the front porch, reasoning that it was better to keep negative energies from entering than to trap them inside the house.

## Review

How to identify places of sadness, suffering, or agitation:

- Find the Stillpoint within.
- Ground, center, and shield.
- Train by using the power of opposites.
- Practice "reading" the energy of places.

# Chapter Two

# Preparing to Liberate Trapped Energies

*Mitakuye oyasin*
<small>LAKOTA PRAYER</small>

Becoming a conduit for liberating trapped energies and clearing spaces to balance and create healthy, healing environments requires recognizing the sacredness inherent in all things. To this end, it is important to realize that all beings are related in a sacred circle of life. Native peoples acknowledge this, evidenced by the fact that their prayers frequently end with the Lakota phrase, *"Mitakuye oyasin,"* which translates as "all my relations"—everything that stands (trees), sits (rocks), creeps, crawls, slithers, swims, flies, or walks, as well as people of all nations on earth and the forces at work in the universe.

The relatedness of everything can be better understood by comprehending that the substance of all beings—whether rock, plant, insect, fish, bird, animal, or human—is actually energy manifesting in consistent patterns as matter. Matter is mostly space held together by a vibration, and the particular ratios of substance are what determine specific forms. Essentially, an object is energy, with its vibration sufficiently slowed down to become a physical manifestation. Although a rock appears to be quite different from a human being, they are both composed not only of largely the same chemistry but also the same particles: electrons, neutrons, protons, and so forth. And because each of the elements of the human body is found in the earth, a handful of dirt is basically a handful of humanity, only it is constellated in a different energetic pattern. Moreover, every object or being has an energy body, or light body, called a MerKaBa, as well as a blueprint that represents its expression in physical form. The MerKaBa is the energetic framework which all beings share and which, based on sacred geometry, forms the blueprint for spirit to attach to and for DNA to create a physical expression from. Further, each being has a spirit—the divine light and creative force that make it a living entity and simultaneously enable its existence on a higher plane independent of the physical world so that, after death, the spirit does not cease to exist but only leaves the physical plane.

All beings have a highest expression of energy that can be attained with guidance from a higher power. The highest expression of your personality, for example, is achieved by merging your thoughts and actions with a higher power. Similarly, when rocks, plants, and animals are connected with their source, they attain the highest expression of their being. Moreover, the earth with its physical features—mountains, rivers, plains, beaches, and so forth—also has a highest expression that can be more closely attuned to; it is called the Christ Consciousness Grid. This grid is an energy layer surrounding the earth and signifying the earth's highest potential. Supposedly established by higher beings (often referred to as Ascended Beings), the grid's purpose is to help humanity through the current "shift of the ages," a major vibrational transformation underway—according to indigenous peoples and a handful of scientific researchers.

When clearing and cleansing structures and lands and transmuting their energy, focusing on the outward expression of matter is less important than concentrating on the essence and energy patterns of beings and objects. Consequently, working energetically with spaces involves relating with the source of life (soul, spirit, *animus*) that allows outward expressions of living beings to occur as coherent patterns in this plane of existence. This means acknowledging the sacred nature of the work, as well as interacting reverently with the spirit of any object, animate or inanimate, for all spirits are one with the Creator. By using your own spirit, or divine light, it is possible to perceive the interaction between an object's blueprint and its divine light, and then to change the energy of that object to enable the expression of its highest potential. In pursuing such energy work, it is wise to be respectful. Just as you wouldn't carelessly tamper with an individual's soul, you should be mindful of the manner in which you engage the energy of a place, a rock, a plant, or an animal. When seeking to use or change its energy, first acknowledge its existing beauty and power and then, with humility and respect, ask permission for change to occur. This approach is common practice in many indigenous societies, including Native American cultures. The goal is to become a "hollow reed," a conduit through which the power of the Creator might flow.

Such an activity is especially important today, when due to the coming "shift of the ages" the vibrational energies of the earth are changing radically. This transformative time is called by some the beginning of the New Age, while others say it will result in "ascension," causing the planet to enter a new dimension. Various authors have written of this "shift of the ages" as a time of accelerated energy, where more is happening more quickly as the "end of time" approaches, predicted by the Mayan calendar to occur in the year 2012. According to Mayan, Hopi, and Aztec views of time and the universe, there have been four worlds, or "suns," of humankind, and we are entering the fifth world—a chronology corroborated by interpretations of the Great Pyramid in Egypt measured as a calendar, by biblical prophecies of the "end times," and by Hindu *yugas*, or cycles of time.

The purpose of individuals presently on earth, according to mystics and seers who rely on these ancient teachings of spiritual guidance, is to recognize personal responsibility to co-create this transformation—that is, to effect goodness in partnership with the Creator while remaining aware of personal limitations of power and wisdom. We are all called to this task at the present time, both individually and collectively. Some people experience it as a pull to become more closely attuned to what Native Americans call the Sacred Hoop of Life, or the interrelatedness of all beings, while others view it as a "coming home" to find a oneness with others and the earth, for the benefit of all. This purpose can be accomplished in energy work by connecting places and lands to the Christ Consciousness Grid, thereby generating greater forces of energy and creating even more potential for the expression of yet higher forms of energy.

## *Ley Lines, Sacred Sites, and the Christ Consciousness Grid*

In preparation for altering the energy of places, it is helpful to gain an overview of the context and configuration of earth's energy patterns and to know what energy types might be encountered. For example, it is important to be informed about the existence of ley lines, sacred sites, and the Christ Consciousness Grid. Ley lines are energy grids that crisscross the earth's surface, holding electromagnetic energy potential in the same way that meridians of energy do as they pass through the human body. Meridians, which have been precisely mapped by practitioners of the ancient arts of Eastern medicine, are used in healing techniques such as acupuncture, which remove blockages so that energies can flow freely to promote well-being.

Ley lines have been recognized as corridors of potential energy and used by various cultures throughout the ages to heighten spiritual awareness. For instance, most old cathedrals and megalithic structures in Europe and many temples and shrines in the Americas were built atop ley lines near sites designated sacred by ancient peoples. Likewise, markings on stones—pictographs or petroglyphs—or circles of stones (ancient medicine wheels or megaliths) often indicate that the structure is on a ley line. Such sites tend to have incredible energetic potential, although it may require activation through ritual or ceremony.

Many sacred sites—such as Chaco Canyon in northwestern New Mexico—are now maintained as state or federal parks, reflecting their enduring attraction. Additionally, the military has recognized the usefulness of natural power spots, for in recent years it has appropriated some of these lands and instigated extensive research into techniques such as remote viewing and transmutation of earth energy with the intent to cause weather changes and influence military maneuvers.[1] Throughout the ages, shamans and adepts of diverse cultures have identified sacred sites as locations in which a permeable energy layer between the earth and upper worlds may be passed through. However, only in recent years has this been recognized as the Christ Consciousness Grid, the energy layer that holds the pattern signifying the highest potential of the earth.

According to sacred geometry, the Christ Consciousness Grid is associated with life force, prana, or ether, and forms a dodecahedron, the most evolved sacred shape before form returns to a blank sphere, or void, from which all shapes derive. It is said that this energy layer above the earth was established over a period of time by the beings of highest spiritual accomplishment. They saw humanity developing toward either transcending physical form or annihilating themselves and the world, and consequently created this grid to function as an archetype inspiring the positive evolution of the world and all beings. When the energy of the grid is brought to the physical plane, all beings and the earth itself are elevated, providing a catalyst for the highest manifestation and ultimate ascension of the earth and all its beings. Though it is said that atomic testing and the beaming of high-frequency waves have nearly negated the grid's effect on the earth, in recent years indigenous medicine men and women around the world have been working extensively to keep the grid active and uninfluenced by the electromagnetic maelstrom produced by modern society. In energy work, connecting buildings and lands to the Christ Consciousness Grid contributes to the potential for higher expressions of energy.

## Water Sources and Embedded Energy

Water sources can pose challenges to the sensing of energy because they sometimes mimic ley lines. Structures are often built above underground streams, which may, unless care is taken, cause disruptions in the energy of the buildings because outside energies can flow in and become embedded in the walls or floor then turn stale, requiring clearing, especially in urban areas or rural areas near toxic-waste dumps. On a positive note, free-flowing clean water under a structure, because of the fresh energy it brings in, constantly flushes out negative energy. For this reason, in some areas of the world, meditative sites are often located near streams. The ancient Chinese practice of Feng Shui, or positioning structures in balance with the energy of a place, employs this movement of "chi," or life-force energy. In fact, in Mandarin, "feng" literally means wind and "shui" water. In Japan, the beautiful pagodas are often perfectly positioned between land forms and water, acknowledging this power of natural energy to promote balance and wholeness.

## *Burial Spots*

Energy work can be required when buildings are constructed atop or adjacent to burial grounds that still hold energy. Such structures may need frequent clearing, although many places thought to be Native American burial mounds exude positive energy of high vibration since they were created along ley lines and also used for ceremonial purposes. Examples of structures built on or near burial grounds include: a Baptist church outside present-day Lake Mills, Wisconsin, built by settlers adjacent to a thousand-year-old burial mound that now serves as the Historical Museum at Aztalan State Park; a church located adjacent to one of the oldest burial mounds in Pocahontas, Mississippi; and, in Mississippi's Delta region, homes built by settlers atop mounds to avoid the destructive effects of flooding. To clear burial spots, it may first be necessary to learn how to deal with ghosts, spirits, and other entities, which requires additional skills.

## Ghosts and Unwanted Entities

Ghost stories abound throughout history, and scary movies are created every year to capitalize on people's fear of death. Old cities in Europe and the Americas often host "ghost walks" to point out areas where sightings have frequently occurred. Ghosts are a part of our lore for a reason: they are a fact of life, even if they are only of the variety that "go bump in the night." Ghosts are energy fragments that can be encountered in locations such as old homes or sites of natural disasters. People can go through their whole lives without consciously seeing a ghost, but once one's perceptions have been heightened to sense energy, the likelihood of confronting one increases.

To comprehend how to deal with ghosts, it is necessary to understand that most so-called ghosts are spirit fragments of dynamic energy which exude that energy within a repeating pattern. The beings from which they originated have already passed on and have no need for them. Such energy fragments have become stuck like tape loops that need to be broken up and released. Removing them is like cleaning cobwebs from a room and can be accomplished with repeated clearings.

Unfortunately, in our culture movies portray such entities in a sinister way, reinforcing fears about them, when in fact we live in a sea of energies—including the souls of the departed—with a wide range of both negative and positive influences. Normally, a soul remains in or revisits the body periodically for seventy-two hours after death. In the practice of Tibetan

Buddhism, it takes that long for a person sitting next to the body to recite the *Tibetan Book of the Dead,* a text to orient the deceased for the journey. Anything said or thought about a person who has just died can be heard by that soul for at least seventy-two hours. Occasionally a soul will linger longer—usually for a few days but sometimes for years or even centuries—and such situations benefit from encouraging the soul to let go of the former existence. Releasing such "lost souls" is called psychopomp.[2] It is not a form of exorcism, or de-possession; rather, psychopomp is the art of lovingly releasing souls who are usually just confused—a specialty with which every healer who deals with death and dying should be familiar, if only to help ensure that the final moments of a person's life may be as peaceful as possible.

Such ghosts may be found either in buildings, especially those where traumatic events have occurred, or out on the land, just as one might come upon a wasp's nest under the eaves. Though their presence is no cause for great alarm, the way to keep these entities from enacting mischief is to maintain a high vibrational rate through clearing and cleansing. Some unsettled energies may actually enter a person's aura, or even their physical body, and although some people are fearful of being possessed by such forces, in fact they generally have very little impact and are not usually threatening to human well-being. However, if a truly negative force manifests, or a lost soul continues to linger, it is best to contact a shaman or someone trained in dealing with such energies.[3]

## Other Beings

Other beings that may be encountered include elementals—variously known by such names as sprites, fairies, and elves—and extraterrestrials, or star beings. Many of these beings, especially elementals, can aid in clearing and cleansing structures and particularly land, if approached in the right way. Elementals attend to the earth's energies and manifestations (such as plants and water), and every culture has a name for them: fairies in the British Isles, "little people" among the Cherokee, *dryads* in Greece, *leshiye* in Russia, *shedim* among Jewish people, *afries* in Egypt, and *yowahoos* elsewhere in Africa. The Findhorn Foundation in Scotland has worked with these beings for thirty years and published books about how they have tended its gardens, from the tiniest elementals working with flowers to the great devas of whole landscapes. But not all sprites, fairies, and elves are content with small chores: some are quite powerful spirits of the land.

Whereas such beings have been stereotyped in popular culture, they are actually quite diverse, in both appearance and function. In Ireland, for example, there are the powerful Tuatha De Danaan, subjects of the Celtic goddess Danu. Although lumped together under the category of fairies or elves, they are believed to be descendants of star beings who populated the earth ages ago and are, maybe not so coincidentally, similar in power and history to the beings ancient Tibetans described as the Lha. The Lha, according to a thirteenth-century account called the *Chojung,* came to earth when it was devoid of vegetation and manifested plants and animals through a form of deep meditation called *samten se,* which they eventually forgot how to do. Most Native American cultures have similar legends about star beings. Even elves, which are portrayed almost comically in popular culture, have a more powerful pedigree. The name derives from the Scandinavian *alfar,* referring to spirits of the mountains, forests, and waters. To perceive such beings, it's best when thinking of them to forget any preconceived notions and to trust instead what you sense or feel.

Elementals have a range of energetic qualities. Some entities with positive energy are beneficial, such as those inhabiting plants and trees. Others with negative energy appear in nightmarish contexts, such as the creatures seen by alcoholics suffering from delirium tremens. Clearing spaces creates an environment to which helpful elementals will be drawn, and from which others will scatter because in energy work like attracts like: negative emotions attract negative entities that feed on them, while positive emotions attract positive energies that boost the overall vibration. That is why in any shamanic practice one must avoid succumbing to fear, which feeds negative entities, making them appear more terrifying and powerful. In fact, most negative entities are usually harmless but know how to create a fearsome appearance to produce the type of energy that will enhance their capabilities. The way to defeat a fear-provoking entity is by generating love or laughter; positive energy is painful and repulsive to negative entities and will cause them to scatter, while enticing positive entities.

Unlike most elementals, extraterrestrials, or star beings, have existed on earth in various forms for thousands of years, according to cultures around the world. They are depicted in petroglyphs in the American Southwest, in cuneiform tablets from Sumeria, in ancient Egyptian frescoes, and among the ruins of civilizations in Central and South America. Our national fascination with stories about the truth or fiction of the 1947 incident at Roswell, New Mexico, and other more recent publicized accounts of "flying saucers," diverts attention from the ongoing existence of star beings on earth. Whether or not they are considered "real" in today's society simply does not matter since they exist independently of our cultural acknowledgment; they were here before us and will probably be here long after we are gone.

Extraterrestrials can alter the energetic environment, so it is important to notice them if they show up. Simply go about your work. Most often they are seen in non-ordinary reality—in trance state—by shamans, seers, mystics, and those who may be open to perceiving reality in altered states caused by drugs, sleep deprivation, or unusual confluences of energy. Sightings of extraterrestrials are usually associated with certain land formations, energy vortices, and powerful natural forces, such as volcanoes, earthquakes, and geomagnetic variations or structures linked to them. For some reason, they seem particularly prevalent in the desert regions of the American Southwest. They are frequently spotted when doing work on land forms, and most seem surprised when seen in the shamanic state.

Despite the sensational depictions of extraterrestrials in popular culture—most of which are driven by fear and ignorance—people should not feel threatened by them. They generally avoid three-dimensional reality, or the "earth plane," and if they do enter it they have a specific reason for doing so and leave thereafter. Most of these beings keep their distance and just want to observe, as our planet is a source of wonder to many species throughout the galaxy. Knowing of the existence of star beings and perhaps developing the expectation and heightened perception to see one helps us strengthen our belief in various realms of energy—especially the usefulness of energy work in a global or universal context, such as work linking buildings and lands to the Christ Consciousness Grid.

## *Portals*

Portals are vortices through which objects and entities can pass from one dimension of reality to another, a phenomenon called "realm shifting." You may have experienced the disappearance of an object from your home or office and wondered where it went. That's a good indication of realm shifting due to the opening of a portal. Realm shifting occurs from time to time where there are high frequency vibrations. Portals, while good for manifesting energies of the past and future, may create problems when entities shift realms and cause events to occur or objects to disappear into another dimension. However, don't be alarmed if items vanish in your home or office as they will generally resurface at some point, sometimes very close to where they were originally. And even though extraterrestrials and other inter-dimensional beings use portals to pass through three-dimensional reality, such entities are usually harmless.

## *Guides, Angels, Goddesses, and Power Animals*

Guides, angels, goddesses, and power animals are all beneficial to individuals and often help with energy work if proper relationships with them can be established. Fortunately, they are becoming popular topics in our culture, a development which helps to counteract the legacy of scary movies.

Although personal guides are always present, whether they are seen or not depends on the needs and wishes of the perceiver. We usually have one guide who accompanies us throughout life and others who come to our aid from time to time, particularly when we make important decisions that will determine our life path. They can be a soul brother or sister—a being close to you in a former or future lifetime—or spiritual masters who have assumed a supportive role during your soul's evolution.

Psychics are the most adept at perceiving their guides. America's well-known clairvoyant, Sylvia Browne, credits her guide, a South American Indian whose name in life was Lena. Dorothy Chitty, a celebrated psychic from England, reports that she has had many guides, including a man in a brown suit whom she thought was

God, a deceased relative named Uncle Charlie, and her main guide today, Li Ching. Non-psychics might catch a glimpse of their guides out the corner of the eye in a dream state, or might simply sense that someone supportive is nearby. If while having a sudden insight you feel someone beside you, it's likely that your guide is there. Most of us are so accustomed to tuning out our surroundings that we delude ourselves into believing that sudden insights are our own; in fact, guides are often the source of second thoughts or sudden inspirations. Guides offer love and assistance in ways that may never be acknowledged or appreciated and can be great teachers whose wisdom aids our development. Sometimes one with a particular expertise will come forward to help with technical aspects we need to learn in order to follow a calling. Entire councils of spiritual elders and celestial orders of light beings can even assist us when requested.

While guides can offer help and counsel, a tremendous source of loving compassion and guidance of a higher order is available through angelic help. Most Westerners are familiar with angels from religious stories, such as accounts in the Bible of angels appearing before incredulous people to give glad tidings—like the three wise men learning of Christ's birth and angels coming to the aid of Daniel in the lion's den. The Koran, too, is filled with accounts of angels, called *Mala'ikah* in Arabic. To believe that angels existed thousands of years ago but not today signifies a subjugation of heart by mind, compassion by ego; some of the most marvelous modern-day sightings of angels are recounted by author

Doreen Virtue. Believed to be made of light energy and capable of materializing into any form, angels exude pure love and bestow wisdom—often when support is least expected and most needed.

Angels' embodiment of light energy allows them to take on diverse roles, many of which have become associated with miracles. They serve as messengers from the Creator to aid us on our life journey, guardians to help us improve our skills and understanding, and dispensers of aid to the spirits of gestating infants. Additionally, they assist in the transmutation of energies, as in a clearing ceremony. We are each born with a "guardian angel," then others come at various times to help with specific tasks or bring new energies, events, or people into our lives, usually by guiding us to them or toward beneficial activities.

Angels assigned specific tasks can help make our lives more purposeful and fulfilling by opening our hearts, for example, or transmuting toxic emotions. We are all "touched" by an angel from time to time; we have only to learn to perceive them. When an angel's presence is sensed, it often feels like being enfolded in love, like soft wings of warm light encircling us and evoking feelings of safety. When an angel is nearby, the light will appear different—more lucid and enlivened—and we may feel tears of joy well up. The key to recognizing the presence of an angel is feelings of gentleness, security, and love, usually accompanied by insights that seem to have a divine source.

Goddess energy is powerful, as well, its effects ranging from the sudden and dramatic to the subtle and long lasting. Some goddesses are connected to a particular place, such as a sacred site, a mountain, or a valley, while others manifest in many places simultaneously and are sufficiently timeless to exist in the past, present, and future.

For personal development and increased creativity, it is advantageous to create spaces where goddesses are inclined to appear, usually areas that have been cleared and cleansed, with high vibrational levels. Goddesses prefer land forms that have the capacity to hold a lot of power, such as mountains, rivers, plains, or quiet woodland groves. But it is not necessary to go to such places to see goddesses. Instead, one can lovingly nurture a space in which they can manifest, such as a sacred fire made of wood carefully selected as gifts of the trees. Goddesses can be seen in the flames and smoke as visions, often small but sometimes rising to great heights. Peoples of various cultures have experienced such fire visions for thousands of years.

The Cherokee, for example, often employ this type of vision, called *Us'ste'lisk* (pronounced oo-stay-leesk), to assist young people in following a medicine path, although anyone can use this method. A sacred space is created by selecting thirteen river stones (stone people) and arranging them in a circle; at its center the fire, made from wood reverently selected, is lit and time is set aside for insights to occur, often preceded by days of fasting. Another way to connect with the energy of goddesses is by creating an altar. It need only be a small space such as the corner of a dresser or a shelf, with an image of a goddess or an emblem—such as a rock, leaf, or twig—that serves as a link to the place where the goddess resides or was once seen. Such an altar can serve as a daily devotional spot and reminder of goddess energy, guidance, and vision. Goddesses are with us always if we desire it and keep our hearts, eyes, and ears open for them to communicate with us.

Everyone is born with a power animal, or totem, that remains with them throughout their lives—an independent operator that offers guidance and protection in different forms, depending on function. For example, when watching over a child it may appear as a cuddly creature, like a teddy bear, but when protecting a child it may manifest as a grizzly bear. In addition to the main totem with which individuals are born, several other power animals will come and go during a lifetime. Each is a power of the universe and can do virtually anything, even intervene if individuals go astray. But their main task is to guide and protect unobserved, communicating through intuition.

According to the visions of shamans, all guides, angels, goddesses, and power animals are located in different levels of existence and are accessed through non-ordinary reality. Typically, shamans of all cultures divide existence into three parts: the lower world, the middle world, and the upper world. The lower world, despite Western ideas about hell, may be conceived of as a world much like the earth, with mountains, meadows, and rivers—a region where power animals reside. The middle world is the earth's surface itself, where we live, which we share with our guides, angels, and goddesses. Although to us it is the realm of ordinary reality, when experienced intuitively by shamans, seers, and visionaries, the middle world is revealed instead as a realm where some places and objects have greater power than others. The upper world is where the highest teachers reside and where we may be accompanied by our guides, angels, goddesses, and power animals. When death occurs, the soul passes into the upper world until it reaches a "crack in the universe," at which point it returns from whence it came. In addition to the three worlds, the earth has many grids superimposed above its surface (just as ley lines crisscross on the surface), forming geometric shapes with various functions. Scientists have mapped some of these grids, such as the Van Allen Belt, while others have been seen by visionaries—such as the grid holding the akashic records, a morphogenic field containing all the lifetimes and potential lifetimes of every living being.

Although shamans and visionaries have special abilities to perceive non-ordinary reality in the three worlds, anyone can develop the capability to "see" the energy of objects and spaces around them, or in other worlds, by increasing their awareness of energy patterns. This is done by acknowledging first of all that what we are capable of seeing or not seeing is taught to us so that our perception is controlled by preconceptions.

In the 1960s, Dr. Timothy Leary conducted experiments with LSD that explored the nature of reality and what really goes on in the human mind, though his bona fide research was overshadowed by the chic motto of "tune in, drop out." (For a fascinating look at how we create and operate from "reality" as it's imprinted on us from childhood and, unless altered, never changes, see his book *Change Your Brain*.) Leary's conclusions were that we form our "reality" based on agreement with others on what constitutes reality and excluding sensory input that doesn't fit this concept. Research over the past few decades has resulted in many new ways of looking at the world, as demonstrated in the film *What the *#Bleep Do We Know?*

As it's now understood, we each have within us a "meta-programmer" that screens out sensory data and projects objects into our visual construct within the brain to make our reality conform to how we are culturally imprinted to perceive it. We overcome such preconceptions of reality by enhancing the capabilities of the senses. If we allow ourselves to see what supposedly cannot be seen, we expand our sensory perception so that over time objects, beings, and energies will be seen not as 3-D reality but in the reality that supersedes and infuses it—namely, non-ordinary reality. This is called "taking the blinders off," and much of the 1960s generation did it through ingesting drugs. But drug use is not required to enhance perception, since the substances considered necessary for psychedelic experiences in the 1960s occur naturally in the brain. While it's important to keep open the doorways of perception, psychedelic drugs blast the doors off their hinges, as opposed to "taking the blinders off" by allowing ourselves to see beyond the consensual view of reality. Often this calls for an ability to pass beyond the boundary of fear, which occurs when we learn to trust our guides, angels, goddesses, and power animals.

To open the door to enhanced perception, practice activating your intuition. If you catch a glimpse of something that appears to be from non-ordinary reality and your mind automatically discounts its existence, return to the image and work with it. In recent years, scientists have begun mapping the physiology of the brain's electrical impulses, revealing that the intuitive sites in the brain that seers, mystics, and shamans use are adjacent to the center for imagination; visioning (see Exercise 2), daydreaming, night dreaming, and guided meditation open these sites. With practice and use, they can be activated in an instant.

### Exercise 2: Visioning

Visioning is a great asset as you prepare to liberate trapped energies, for it helps you attune to your intuition, your core sense of knowing. To begin visioning, lie down in a quiet place free of distractions. Once you are comfortable, close your eyes and focus on your breathing. As thoughts enter your mind one by one refocus on your breathing until all the inner "voices" are stilled. It might be helpful to play soft music, perhaps a tape of Native drumming or the soothing sounds of crystal bowls.

In this relaxed state, imagine a place you know well, and in your mind visit this place. If it is a room in your home, for instance, see and feel yourself there. Notice the scent in the air. Looking around, observe the arrangement of chairs, tables, and other furniture. What sense do you make of the objects in the room? Are some intricate and detailed, or fuzzy and hard to see? Let the objects show themselves to you, revealing features you have not yet noticed.

Enjoy your visit thoroughly, then open your eyes and write down what you saw while visualizing, recalling as many details as possible. As soon as you can, actually go to the place and examine it carefully. You may find that some objects were omitted from your visualizing whereas others are smaller or larger than those you saw. Repeat this exercise until you really "know" the place—and are able to delight in the differences between its physical reality and your inner sense of it.

Once you have gained proficiency in visioning, apply it to other places in your world. With practice, you will be able to see more of the reality in your midst because your intuition, or "second sight," will be increasingly operative. You may even have the opportunity to see and greet your guides, angels, goddesses, and power animals.

# *From the Energy Notebook: The Power of Dreaming*

You can further prepare to liberate trapped energies by learning how to let your dreams direct you to places of power and insight that may assist personal growth and thus facilitate your energy work. For example, in spring 2003 I had a powerful dream that changed my life, with the help of the energies and entities of a place. I saw myself at my favorite spot on earth—the summit of Black Mesa, a 5,000-foot rise where Oklahoma, New Mexico, and Colorado meet. There my wolf power animal, with a wolf companion, loped toward me, grinning mischievously. As I watched from above, in spirit, he and his companion proceeded to tear my body apart and devour me, chewing my bones then regurgitating my remains. After my wolf loped off, I continued to watch the bloody pile of my remains, with my heart still beating. As the seasons changed, I saw grass sprouting up around my heart in spring, the sun beating down on it in summer, leaves blowing across it in autumn, and steam rising off it as frigid winter winds howled. Then I heard a voice say, "You will find your heart at Black Mesa."

After repeated dreams of being at the mesa with the wolves and watching my heart beating, I knew I had to do a spirit quest—a journey devoted to following only what Spirit dictates—at Black Mesa. Before I went, I was told in a dream, "You will go up the mesa with two hearts and come down with one." It was true. I traveled to Black Mesa when I was wrestling with many things and thus had "two hearts." I spent four days at the mesa, where I came to know the spirits of the land: hearing the voice of Spirit in the wind, crying tears like rain, thinking thoughts like thunder, gaining insights like lightning, hearing my own voice echoing back from the land as the very voice of God.

Focusing only on the entities of the place and the energy of the land forms, I "became" one with the wind, rocks, and trees. I could feel the golden rays of the sun showering me with light. The colors of the place were so vibrant as to be empowering; the sky, for example, was not just the color blue but its vibration. The stones, though lacking eyes and ears and mouths, were eloquent in their communication and of such power that they spoke directly to my heart, telling stories of the ages when we were one. The silence of the desert was filled with wisdom beyond that which one mind alone could fathom.

It was as if every fiber of my being was absorbing the power and purity of the place. My spirit was broken into a thousand shards—shared with rocks, sky, plants, birds, the air—and reformed as a new being, transformed in a sacred way with a timeless kinship to all beings. By seeing the divinity in all things, I saw my own divinity and came to know that all life shares this sacredness with the Creator.

As I was coming down from the mesa on the last day, I heard the voice of an ally, a powerful spirit of nature capable of helping if asked. My attention was drawn to a small stone in the shape of a wolf's head. Realizing that I had gone up the mesa with two wolves, opposing forces, eating at me, and had come down with one, I thanked the ally for this gift.

Another vision I had while in a dream state occurred during a spirit quest in the desert on Hopi land. As I lay all night on a blanket beneath the moon and stars between waking and dreaming, I had a powerful vision in which one by one the *kachinas*—supernatural beings revered by the Hopis as messengers from the spirit world—showed me where they came from and how I could call on them in times of need, giving insights and blessings. Such experiences have impressed on me the value of being conscious of powerful dreams and using their content to gain insights and enhance intuition in life.

Dreams can guide you along your life's path or lead to places where the spirits of the land may become your allies. By embracing these opportunities for growth, our life purposes grow more sharply delineated. Everyone dreams, and through persistent intent everyone can learn to employ their content advantageously for greater understanding of the self and spirit life. To improve the recollection of dreams and the beneficial use of their content, keep a notepad by your bed, and just before going to sleep resolve to remember all dreams and write them down immediately upon waking. Over time, not only will you automatically begin recalling dreams but you will consciously participate in them, thus gaining more insight into their meaning and increasing power over your consciousness. To do this, apply the simple yet effective technique taught to Carlos Castaneda by his teacher, Don Juan: while in a dream state, remember to look for your hands, because when you find them you can control the dream.[4] Mastering this power can then lead to other abilities, including conversing with the spirits of the land.

## Review

How to prepare to liberate trapped energies:
- Respect the sacredness of all things.
- Ask what needs to be done, rather than indiscriminately imposing your will.
- Trust in guides, angels, goddesses, and power animals to direct and protect your efforts.
- Employ dream visions to aid you.

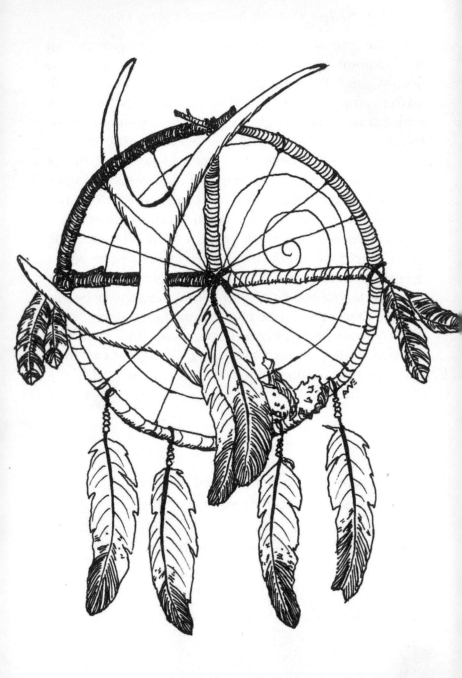

## Chapter Three

# Meeting the Spirits of the Land

*Namasté*

*(The divinity within me salutes the divinity
within you)*

SANSKRIT GREETING

In respecting and thanking the earth and its spirits for abundance and miracles, good intentions are reinforced, the earth's beings are empowered to optimally express their divinity, and a reciprocal rejuvenation of spirit occurs. Just as a person glows when acknowledged with respect and gratitude, intensifying positive energy in the surroundings, the land also responds energetically to gestures of appreciation.

Often, when I have done ceremonies at various places, the spirits of the land will leave gifts. For example, after a ceremony by the seashore interacting with the spirits of the water and land, I picked up my blanket and found a beautiful seagull feather. Another time following a ceremony in the mountains, beside my medicine bag was a perfectly shaped quartz crystal from "out of nowhere." And one day while leaving a building that had required extensive work, I looked up to see a magnificent rainbow arcing across the sky.

Meeting the spirits of the land involves praying with the whole self—body, mind, and spirit—to connect with the divine source of our being and awaken the spirits by acknowledging their presence. Ceremonies evolving out of such meetings cause natural energies to flourish.

The spirits of the land are present all the time, if only people would be open to sensing and seeing them and knew how to activate them. In ancient times, every culture had deities connected with the land that could be perceived as clearly as we today would identify a well-known personality on TV or in the movies. For example, though someone may have never met a celebrity icon like Marilyn Monroe, through pop culture that person would immediately recognize images of her and know many intimate details of her life, even though she's been dead for forty years.

Likewise, the energy of deities exists forever in the collective memory of the human race because energy cannot be destroyed, only transmuted. Once intent manifests patterns of energy, unless they are transformed they continue to exist, if only potentially. Enduring archetypes of gods and goddesses linked to nature include: in Native American culture, the Corn Maiden, who offers sustenance; in British culture, the Green Man, who makes things grow; and in Egyptian mythology, Osiris, god of the yearly regeneration of vegetation in spring. Each has a function corresponding to a human need, and expressed in a form that varies from culture to culture.

Recognizing the energetic potential of a place to manifest spiritual beings and accentuating the senses are the means to meeting the spirits of the land. For example, people's use of perception beyond visual sight and willingness to be open to spirits are the reasons Ix Chel still exists for Mayan peoples as a living goddess and Quan Yin lives on as a bodhisattva for Chinese Buddhists. When places are approached in a sacred manner, with the intention of seeking guidance to be an agent of Spirit, the corresponding energy manifests such deities. If prejudice exists against the possibility of encountering deities, it is doubtful their presence will be sensed.

Prejudice against the possibility of meeting the spirits of the land can be the result of many conditions. Two principal ones are the belief in modern societies that tangibility defines reality—that what cannot be seen or touched is not real—and the tendency in all societies to define reality by consensus. For example, when the first Europeans arrived in the Americas, it is said that the indigenous peoples could not see the large, wooden ships anchored at their shores because such objects didn't exist within their frame of reality. A shaman saw ripples in the water, however, after which he could see the ships, and then the people could see them, too. The ripples from the rocking ships informed him that "something" was different. That is, allowing for other possibilities, expanding his frame of reference, and taking his "blinders" off, he eventually was able to "see" the ships. Once he saw them, bringing the images into his own consciousness, the entire tribe was able to view the "reality" of the ships, as well. Similarly, to meet the spirits of the land, we are tasked with having to "see."

Being aware of the existence of other forms of energy, such as deities, allows them to manifest as visual phenomena. Just as children learn to see squiggly lines on a page as words, by being open to patterns of energy that are subtly present and believing that they can be associated with deities, people can learn to see the spirits of the land. Also, if an object or idea exists in the consciousness of some people it has the potential to become a reality for a greater number of people. Often, all it takes is for someone to point it out. Until such an enlightening moment occurs, a UFO may be mistaken for a cloud, and a natural spirit for a thin mist.

The power of collective intention can be even stronger, manifesting old patterns of energy. Deities that may not have manifested for hundreds or thousands of years, so-called slumbering goddesses, may reappear in response to just the right circumstances and intentions of large numbers of people—for example when, every twelve years, during the festival of Kumbha Mela, millions of Hindus gather at the confluence of the Ganges and Jumna rivers in India to manifest miracles.

Such manifestations occur especially when the land's vibrational level is high—due either to intrinsic conditions (such as the proximity of ley lines) or when the vibrational level has been elevated by collective intent. Collective intent occurring in a place of positive energies dissipates negative energies and promotes loving respect for all beings.

## *Perceiving Divine Energies*

To open the way for encounters with the spirits of the land, it is essential to believe in their existence and their great potential for helping humans to live more creative and healthy balanced lives. These spirits appear in various forms and can be perceived by any of the senses. Yet, because they don't normally exist in three-dimensional reality—because we have not opened our perception to them—what is seen, felt, and heard is often indirect. Sometimes their forms appear in smoke rising from a campfire, or their voices may be heard in the wind. They may manifest as a touch felt on the skin, or perhaps simply as a "knowing." Their messages can be perceived through activities of nature, such as a bird flying overhead or a wave slapping water. However, because they cannot be sensed until habitual patterns of perception have been transcended, it is necessary to quiet the internal dialogue that dictates what can and cannot be seen. Then the spirits can communicate directly to your inner realms, through intuition or flights of imagination.

To realize both that learned reality is just a part of total reality and that it is essential to transcend habitual perception to sense divine energies, remember how you saw when you were a child, before your beliefs and habits of seeing became solidified. Recall how alive your surroundings were and the wonder you felt at your constant new discoveries, how you had both real and imaginary friends, and how animals had names and personalities. Once again, allow yourself to see the world in this vivid and animated way by setting aside prejudices that restrict the potential for perception.

In addition, be aware that it is society's conditioning that causes individuals to be judgmental—to see one thing as good and another thing as bad. By contrast, for the Creator no such polarities exist, because to the Creator, all things have equal value: the life of a bug, a tiger, a flower, and a human being is equally precious since each is full of the Creator's love. So when a medicine man causes rain by doodling with a bug, he is tapping into the power and love of the Creator, knowing that the cloud, the bug, the human, and the earth are all one.

Consequently, we can more easily meet the spirits of the land when we stop perceiving only what's inside our heads, conditioned by society, and learn to see with our hearts and whole bodies. When the inner world reflects the outer world, there is greater attainment to the entire spectrum of energy.

## Finding Wild Spirits, or Allies

Allies are easily found, especially if you look for them and are open enough to perceive them in wild places such as prairies, deserts, forests, mountains, and locations where water meets land. For millennia, shamans have gone into the wilderness to seek allies, including rock, tree, plant, and water spirits, because noises produced by humanity are inhospitable to spirit manifestation and allies are more easily perceived in their own elements. When wild places are disturbed or damaged—by water pollution, the cutting down of trees, the leveling of mountains, and so forth—the earth suffers and living beings are harmed. Since the earth's environment continues to be so despoiled by humans, the power, appearance, and numbers of these wild spirits have diminished. By contrast, when wild places are energetically uplifted—for example, through honoring them—the spirits are invigorated and the harmful effects of human destruction can, at least partially, be offset. However, it is not necessary to go far into the wilderness to perceive allies—just out of the mainstream of mechanized living.

Invoking the presence of allies requires a proper attitude since the energetic patterns of these spirits are not strong enough to stabilize as material forms in the intense three-dimensional world and thus require an environment that permits their manifestation. They are brought into this plane by an exchange of energy; that is, people lend them receptive (feminine) energy so that they may reveal their expressive (masculine) energy. Allies manifest by being imprinted on the consciousness of the one seeking them, although today this is virtually a lost art.

Nowadays, people can access information by looking it up in a book or on the Internet. In times past, people asked allies for answers, recognizing that these beings were the caretakers of a vast storehouse of knowledge. For example, allies were used to locate plants for the treatment of diseases or for ceremonial purposes. This is apparently the way in which Amazonian shamans acquired information about the properties of the plant ayahuasca. When people question how they knew of the hallucinogenic properties of this plant among eighty thousand other species, and that it would enable them to have visions, the shamans answer, "The plants told us."

With practice allies can be readily understood since they make unmistakable noises. They sound "natural" but slightly out of character with the landscape and are thus noticeable to the observant. For instance, forest allies—which can be found from the deepest jungle to the quiet groves in a park—frequently make a sound like "tock (pause) tock-tock." Australian Aborigines, as well as indigenous peoples of the rain forest in South America, make "click sticks" that mimic this sound, to attract them. In desert areas and prairies, allies can be found making a sound like the buzzing of an insect, but much louder; Aborigines and some tribes in America's Southwest desert make flat sticks on strings that, when rapidly swung, mimic this sound to help in producing rain. Sometimes allies sound like the wind. You will know when an ally draws near because the hairs on the back of your neck will stand up, your senses will be intensified, and you may feel fear.

When encountering allies, your attitude and emotion can determine their ability or willingness to help. Even though you may feel fear when seeing one—and it's perfectly natural to react in that way as it's an automatic response of the nervous system —fear is the wrong emotion to attract or keep an ally since fear is negative energy that can repel or even anger it. In shamanic terms, this feeling is not actually fear but rather a tightening of the energetic cords in our bodies that bind us to reality. However, the reaction of the rational mind sends the energy of fear like a sword that can cut and hurt, and this is what repels and angers the ally. To avoid this, when feeling the approach of an ally shift your consciousness to your heart, which knows only love. This will attract the ally so that you may befriend it and ask it for help, if you desire.

Allies come to humans because they are interested in them and want to help; they find enrichment by seeing themselves reflected in humans and thus adopt human behaviors. For those reasons, sorcerers have for millennia sought to capture and use allies. They do this by imprinting their thoughts on them so that they carry out the sorcerer's intention. But there are dangers associated with this process. First, since it requires personal power to capture and keep an ally, the ego erroneously assumes that the ally "belongs" to the sorcerer. Second, if allies discern that their power is being misused or limited, they can make life difficult for the one misusing them. It's better, upon finding an ally in the wild, to operate from the heart and allow the ally freedom so that it becomes a true ally—with a mutually beneficial sharing of energy. The goal, in clearing and cleansing your land, is to greet allies without fear, show them your gratitude, and honor them for the work they do to keep the land vital, filled with spirit. In this way, allies can be "used" as powerful forces for harmony in the environment, repelling harm, increasing the vibration rate of plants and animals, and serving as guardians.

In preparation for interacting with allies for mutual benefit, practice shifting consciousness to the heart in nightly prayers by focusing on images and feelings in the heart instead of verbalizing them. Not only will the prayers themselves have more power, but your ability to transmute energy in buildings and on lands will be improved.

## *Discovering Power Animals*

Having a power animal, or totem, is beneficial to clearing and cleansing land and structures through transmutation of energy, since they function as guiding and protecting intermediaries. Individuals can have several power animals at a time, although most people have one, along with other spiritual helpers capable of fulfilling a similar role. You can discover such an animal yourself, perhaps through meditation, or you can ask assistance from someone trained in shamanism. The Foundation for Shamanic Studies holds classes around the country to train people to see, find, and retrieve power animals.[1] Although non-ordinary reality is filtered out by normal consciousness, it may be accessed through drumming, dance, rattling, breathwork, or some other skillful means of inducing a visioning state—an activity which shamans have been performing for about thirty thousand years.

Because power animals resemble a person's strengths and weaknesses, yearnings and limitations, an important way to identify your power animal or animals is by becoming aware of your unique qualities and conscious or subconscious desires. This is sometimes facilitated by recalling childhood identifications with animals, as well as by reviewing major turning points in your life. As a child, there may have been certain animals with whom you felt a special kinship. Later in life, you may have felt an unusual attraction to an animal's qualities because of specific events—perhaps the soaring of an eagle or the grouchiness of a bear.

Further, to identify your power animal, start noticing which creatures repeatedly grab your attention and seem to "speak" to some part of you, including those on television, such as sharks or lions. Even if you can't identify your power animal, it may be instantly obvious to friends and family members. One woman who said she hadn't the foggiest notion what her power animal might be had nearly two hundred turtles on a shelf by her front door—of all shapes, colors, sizes, and materials. She said, "I liked them when I was a little girl, and for some reason people have given them to me all my life."

Once you start to resonate with an animal, reinforce the connection by honoring it. Put a picture of it on the refrigerator or on your desk at work. Create a special ceremony through dance or song, embracing and offering thanks to the animal for appearing. Become "as one" with the animal, as you blend and see through its eyes. Perhaps, in either day or night dreaming, the animal will appear and offer guidance. Power animals can be used in nightly prayers, as well. For example, if a loved one is sick or you are worried about a family member who is far away, ask your power animal to help the individual. You may be surprised by the result, perhaps soon getting a phone call from that person.

After you have connected with your power animal and received guidance, perhaps in the form of a strong intuition, it will be easier to go to your power animal for further counsel as needed. A way to do this is simply to ask your power animal for an answer to a question, and see where or how you are guided. It may be that suddenly your attention is drawn to a phrase in a book that jumps out at you as a clue; or someone may call unexpectedly to offer the help needed; or a chance remark in conversation with someone will reveal an answer to your question. By practicing dialogue with your power animal during the day, in nightly prayers, and through meditation or dreaming, you will become attuned to the power animal and will actually feel its presence with you wherever you go, as reflected in the people, places, and things with which you associate.

## Recognizing Goddesses and Other Local Deities

Compared with power animals, goddesses and other long-established local deities—such as *kachinas*, the spirit messengers of the Hopis—are more elusive. They can appear anytime, anywhere, but it may take some searching to find where they reside. To discover their possible locations, pay attention to intuitive hints, keep your sixth sense attuned to variations in your energetic surroundings, and resist the temptation to rely on what you think you know about a place. For example, just because a lake or unusual land form is surrounded by city or suburban clutter don't assume it's unsuitable for goddesses, who can maintain pockets of non-ordinary reality in the midst of urban blight and remain imperceptible to people not open to seeing them. As in Brigadoon, the mythical place on the Scottish moors that appeared for a single day every hundred years, beneath the pavement and between the buildings in today's world, there is real land with earth energy and even ley lines that can attract goddesses. Of course, locations with the most natural flora and fauna offer the best opportunities to find the reposing place of an ancient slumbering goddess, like a Sleeping Beauty resting in a cocoon of natural energy, awaiting your "kiss" of consciousness.

Such deities are frequently found on sacred lands, some of which are presently threatened by urban sprawl, tourism, or commercial mining. When tribes of indigenous peoples try to prevent mineral extraction on their lands, they are attempting to maintain the sacredness of these places and the energy of deities connected with them, but without more public awareness and support for the concept of sacred sites such battles will certainly be lost.[2] Goddesses found on these sites and elsewhere are powerful, multi-dimensional beings able to shape-shift into various forms and appear simultaneously in different places. They perform miracles, reveal visions, empower individuals, and cause natural phenomena—such as providing rain to parched areas or diverting floods. When you discover a goddess and raise the energy of a site, you empower that goddess—giving her your "kiss" of consciousness—and simultaneously establish a connection with her that encourages her at any time to help you in your tasks. So, finding one goddess has a domino effect, promoting the possibility of finding goddesses in other sacred sites that need elevated levels of vibrational frequency.

Goddesses override all the other orders of natural spirits in a place and are beings with magnitudes greater than elementals, sprites, fairies, and so forth. Goddess energy fortifies the elementals, enriches the landscape, enlivens the plants and animals, and keeps subtle energies flowing. You can recognize a place where a goddess is active because it will have a vibrancy that other places lack: the vegetation will appear greener, the water clearer, the air crisper, and the energy will reflect human emotion—with shadows cast upon the land by angry thoughts, or sunshine appearing with happiness—while simultaneously serving as a buffer to harmful influences.

After discovering a locality where there is goddess energy, the next step is to discern if it is slumbering—that is, simply existing in a pocket within an urban landscape with just enough energy for protection—or if it is flourishing. If the former is true, then it's your task to raise the vibrational rate of the place to empower the goddess and perhaps have her appear to you; if the latter, you might boost the energy to keep the goddess happy and empowered. Since goddesses are no longer generally enlivened by people's energies as they were in times past, their energies have decreased.

Empowered goddesses are "source" beings enlivening everything around them and drawing strength from their own activities. In a sense, they are like the self-sustaining, life-giving properties of the earth itself with its cycles of weather patterns and seasons that maintain conditions for life and growth. Moreover, empowered goddesses can transmute negative energy into life-sustaining energy. They thrive on this energy, spreading its positive effects. And the more powerful they are, the more negative energy they can transmute. So, raising the vibrational rate of a place where a goddess resides can amplify positive energy exponentially and multi-dimensionally. Merely creating an altar in your home featuring an activated goddess—such as Quan Yin, Ix Chel, or the Corn Maiden—can raise the vibration rate of your home and thus invite the goddess to live there, as well as creating positive energy for sustaining her presence.

Although seeing the effects of goddesses is not difficult, identifying them can be problematic since the same one can appear in various forms. For example Quan Yin, an Eastern goddess of compassion, is associated with Isis of ancient Egypt and is known as Kannon in Japan, Kanin in Bali, and Tara in Tibet. She is considered a feminine aspect of Avalokiteshvara, in Sanskrit; Shakti, the wife of Vishnu, in Hinduism; and of the same vibration as Mary, the mother of Jesus. Her signature function, to hear the suffering of the world, is one of the oldest aspects of feminine divinity, occurring in such Gnostic texts as Sophia and associated with yin, or female power (the balance to yang, or male power), the mother of all things. Further, she often shape-shifts into inconspicuous forms while still having a positive influence on people's lives; the "Universal Gateway" chapter in the Lotus Sutra lists thirty-two typical forms in which she may appear.

In many cultures, goddesses are associated with miracles. For instance, there are numerous stories of Quan Yin's miracles in the East over the past millennium, just as there are for the Virgin Mary in the West, as well as numerous tales of blessings bestowed by other goddesses, such as Ix Chel in Central America, Sedna among the Inuit, and White Shell (or White Bead) Woman, of the American Southwest. They take many forms worldwide: for example, the Corn Maiden and Rainbow Woman of the American Southwest are seen as Inkosazana and Mbaba Mwana Waresa respectively by the Zulus of Africa. There is even the Triple Goddess, a motif common to all cultures throughout the centuries, who appears as a maiden, a mature woman, or a crone and teaches that feminine power comes in all forms and is eternal. In fact, the 1,700-year-old Nag Hammadhi texts contain an account of such female power as the alpha and omega of life itself. This Gnostic book, called *The Thunder: Perfect Mind,* posits that God the Creator was female, activated from the virgin void male state of primal nothingness, and upon assuming force, gave birth to all creation, epitomizing the Greek notion of cosmic *pneuma*, the active, intelligent element in all things, made of air and fire. Today, anthropologists and historians are beginning to agree that the patriarchal godhead of modern times is an aberration since ancient peoples worshipped the divine female principle and saw a triumvirate of female, male, and child—not father, son, and holy ghost, which is a notion that arose from the Roman influence of early Christianity and wasn't codified as church doctrine until the fifth century.[3]

Worldwide, there is a goddess for virtually everything, although their types can be quite specific—such as Tei Tituaabine, the "Mother of Trees" in the Gilbert Islands, or the "Mother of Yams" honored and worshipped by the Ibo people of Africa—some only waiting to be born again. As in the movie *Field of Dreams*, where the Kevin Costner character builds a baseball field to attract the spirits of forgotten great players, raising the vibration rate of places, honoring goddesses, and allowing yourself to perceive them encourages goddesses to be present and bestow blessings. By being open to the spirits of a place, personal intent is aligned with the Creator's will, and one becomes a co-creator, acting in the best interest of all.

## Requesting Assistance from Divine Beings and Power Animals

After meeting the spirits of the land, the next step is learning how to ask for their guidance in transmuting energy. Although the Creator invoked the existence of divine beings and power animals to function as caretakers, unless people ask them for help these powers of the universe are generally prevented from intervening. This is because free will, given to individuals to facilitate the learning experiences necessary for evolution, takes precedence.

Before proceeding to assess places or do energy work, then, it is important to ask for help. Requests are best stated as affirmations, since simply asking leaves open the possibility that no answer will be forthcoming. This can be done with the affirmation: "Creator, Earthly Mother, Heavenly Father, Guides, Angels, and Power Animals, thank you for guiding me and protecting me, giving me light so that I can see what I must do." When honored this way, deities and power animals might return the honor, embodying the Sanskrit greeting *namasté*, and grant guidance. By operating from the heart, with faith and pure intention of doing the Creator's will, an individual gains access to greater insights, new modes of perception open up, and there is more potential for the unfolding of miracles.

When entering a place to be cleared or cleansed, it is therefore best to consult your intuition (see Exercise 3), take a moment for prayer (see Exercise 4), and use affirmation to request assistance. Thanking the energies of the place sends the message that you are there to do the highest good for all. You can voice the affirmation while grounding, centering, and shielding in preparation for the energy work. After accessing the Stillpoint, know that you are not alone—your guides, angels, goddesses, and power animals are with you—and that you are working in concert with the spirits of the land. Then in proceeding with a ceremony, you have only to stay present and heed your intuition.

## Exercise 3: Mapping Your Intuition

When looking for a likely place to encounter the spirits of the land, open an atlas of where you reside, an area you plan to visit, or a random location. Then set an intention that your guides and angels show you where you might encounter the spirits of the land. Try to "read" information from these sources by running your hand over the atlas page and noticing areas that transmit a sensation, as the palms of the hand have chakras very sensitive to energy.

Another way to detect likely locations is through the use of a pendulum made of crystals attached to a chain or of a ring tied to a twelve-inch string. Dangle the pendulum, asking it to show directional movements for yes and no, and it will swing one way for yes and the other way for no. Then, holding the pendulum over the locations on the map, frame questions that can be answered by these directional movements: for instance, "Is this a place I should visit?" Gradually refine your questions until you receive very specific answers about locations. You may be guided to places that could not have been found otherwise, without a lot of research, such as power spots known only to the people who reside there. In addition to working directly with maps, follow up on any "niggling" feeling about a place, especially if it keeps coming up in conversation. Establishing an intention and being open to intuition are the keys to pinpointing locations for possible encounters with the spirits of the land.

## Exercise 4: Praying from the Heart

Working with raising the vibration rate of buildings and lands requires working from the heart—not the mind, our customary frame of reference. One way to become more heart centered is through nightly prayers. That is, when going to sleep at night, instead of listing in your mind the people, places, or things you wish to pray for, and then verbalizing your prayers, try visualizing them with your heart.

To begin, think of a person to whom you wish to send blessings for healing or help, then feel what "comes up." Identify the feelings and examine them, sending the individual only the energy of love.

Also explore the images and colors that arise, while allowing them to float before you. You may see, for instance, a golden glow of energy emanating from you, or perhaps deep purple imagery welling up inside you. Understand that gold often represents soothing energy, whereas purple signifies healing forces, and green signifies growth.

As the flow of emotions and colors interacts with the images, you may gain insights into the person's situation or simply feel a release of energy from your heart to theirs. Despite such outpourings of energy, the heart is always full. You will therefore receive as much love as you give, replenishing yourself as you help others.

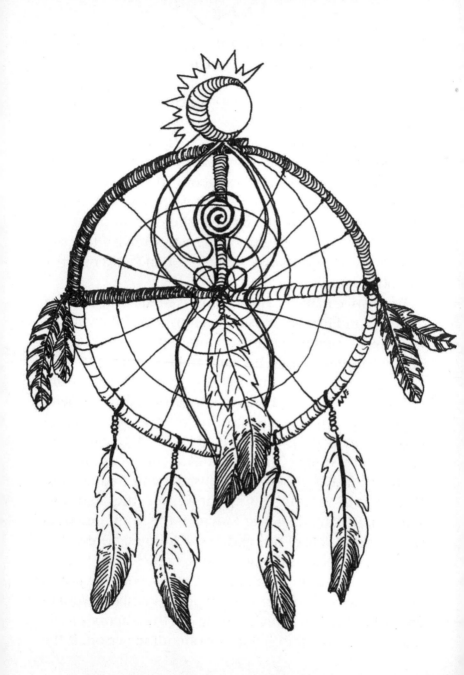

# From the Energy Notebook:
# Following a "Niggling" Feeling

For years there was something "niggling" me about Hot Springs National Park, Arkansas. It seemed every time I turned around there was a reference to this place: it jumped out at me on road maps; friends mentioned it; someone had just been or was about to go there. When traveling, I would suddenly begin musing about the place, but would consider going there an unnecessary detour. Finally, I heeded my inner voice to visit this site and had the miraculous experience of encountering the Rainbow Woman.

The Native name of Hot Springs is Manataka, or Place of Peace, and for centuries its healing waters drew many tribes, who were pledged to maintain peace while there. The hot springs caused the land to be shrouded in mist year round, casting rainbows that could be seen from miles away. The land was confiscated by the federal government in 1832 and turned over to the national park system in 1921, becoming the second national park after Yellowstone. The Manataka American Indian Council (MAIC) preserves the history and traditions of this sacred site, including honoring the Rainbow Woman. Lee Standing Bear Moore of the MAIC describes the historical role of this goddess as follows: "Dressed in all white buckskin and holding one eagle feather in each hand, she stood on the mountain overseeing the peace. When quarrels did arise, a vision of the Rainbow Woman could be seen at twilight rising in the vapors of the highest pool as a warning to the offending person. If the guilty one did not listen to this warning, the Lady of the Rainbow came to him and dropped one feather at his feet, which meant it would be wiser to fly away than to disturb the peace again. If this warning was not heeded, she dropped the second feather as a sign to his family and others to remove the offender from the valley by whatever means necessary."[4]

When I first encountered the Rainbow Woman, I was with a group around a campfire, and the radiant figure appeared to me in the smoke, emanating colors like a prism. At first I couldn't believe my eyes, but when I looked again, thinking the image would be gone, she was still there, gazing directly at me. The goddess saw into my heart and heard my thoughts. When I walked around the fire and stood behind the others, I could see her through the people as if they were made of smoke and only she were real. Seemingly delighted that I could see and hear her, she answered my questions as they formed in my mind. I felt as if my heart had wings of love brought forth from the heat of the fire.

The words the goddess spoke were like musical notes trilling my soul. She told me a great truth: that I must pursue a life of spirit if I wished to fulfill my soul's purpose on earth. She also instructed me to practice the wisdom of the Native American medicine wheel; to understand that while people come from various directions reflecting the wheel's colors—red, yellow, black, and white—they are all one; to comprehend that all people share the heart, or soul, in the center of the wheel. Only by living in this way, honoring all and seeing sameness and not differences, would I truly follow my path. Further, she informed me that I had to speak my truth fearlessly and that my words would find their mark in the hearts of those who can hear her song.

Since I met the Rainbow Woman, I have revisited Hot Springs National Park many times and had long conversations with her, both while awake and while dreaming. It was only through following a "niggling" feeling that I found her and was blessed.

## From the Energy Notebook: Drumming Up the Sun

Wherever I travel, and whether I'm in a hotel room or out in the country, I pay my respects to the spirits of the land by "drumming up the sun." I do this by rising just before dawn, burning sage, and offering a prayer to the four directions. I express gratitude to the Heavenly Father above and the Earthly Mother below. Then I softly beat a drum to get a feel for the earth energies of the place and to tell the local spirits that I come in peace and would be grateful for any help. Such honoring of the local spirits often results in amazing responses, translated by a sense of "knowing." Afterward, I usually write down what I perceived and let it guide me for the day.

For example, once while visiting the Gulf Coast I went out to "drum up the sun" and noticed a pipe protruding from the water, which I ignored. A moment later, a big wave hit the pipe, causing the water to splash me in the face. That evening, I looked at a modern translation of the ancient Mayan calendar and saw that the energy for that day recommended that spiritual guidance be allowed to flow through one like a garden hose and not a steel pipe. I laughed, recollecting the message the spirit of the water had given me.

Another time, in Crestone, Colorado, I went out at dawn to "drum up the sun" and, when I reached a moment in which all things seemed connected, I saw a flying eagle disappear into a cloud over a mountain a short distance away. I couldn't fathom what this meant until later when, while packing to leave, I discovered that the battery in my truck was dead and realized that the message was perhaps that there was still much to be experienced in that place. Indeed, upon extending my visit I became acquainted with fascinating people and met the spirits of the land. I knew it was time to get my truck fixed and go when a few days later, while again "drumming up the sun," I saw another eagle flying from the mountain, which I later learned was Mount Alba, revered by the Navajo people.

This is how the spirits of the land speak—not always through a dramatic vision but through animals, insights, and images that convey clear and powerful messages if we have the patience and insight to comprehend them.

## Review

How to meet the spirits of the land:

- Recognize that they are around you all the time.
- Go to places you are drawn to.
- Ask for the spirits' guidance and help.
- Heed your intuition.

## Chapter Four

# Performing Release Ceremonies

*In nature's infinite book of secrecy,*
*a little I can read.*

WILLIAM SHAKESPEARE,
ANTHONY AND CLEOPATRA

The performance of release ceremonies is a useful means of transmuting energy for healthier and happier living. Living or working in places with negative or stale energy has a long-term destructive impact on one's quality of life in general, as well as on creativity and productivity. Although the impact is often not well understood in our society due to lack of information about the power and forms of energy, it nevertheless plays an important role in people's daily lives. Therefore, the advantages of learning techniques for clearing and cleansing places and land are significant. Use of these tools can result in a more inspired and joyful life.

## *Indoor Spaces*

Any indoor space routinely used for a particular purpose will have organized patterns of thought forms within it. By performing release ceremonies to break up this energy with good intention, through rattling and smudging, it is possible to transmute it to a more positive form, raising its vibrational level.[1] For optimal balance, abundance, and creativity, perform such ceremonies regularly, just as you would routinely clean your home.

## Items Needed to Clear and Cleanse Indoor Spaces

**Rattle.** Any type of rattle will do, even an improvised one consisting of a few small crystals in a pill bottle or some pebbles in a plastic drink container, or in a pinch a bottle of aspirin.

**Smudge stick.** White sage, which is especially good for smudging, can be purchased at specialty bookstores or at powwows, or you can gather it yourself. If you decide to buy a smudge stick, read the label or inquire if the sage was gathered in a sacred manner. If it wasn't, look elsewhere. The land in the western United States is being denuded of sage and other plants by people whose sole intent is profit, with little regard for the plants' sacredness. When plants are gathered without respect, their power is impaired. Cedar, sweetgrass, and incense may also be used, especially if they have been consecrated.[2] This can be done by holding your hands over the plants or incense, and invoking a pure intention, thereby empowering the substances to transmute any toxins that may be present.

*Note:* Some lands have fire restrictions, including even the lighting of a match. If for any reason smoke isn't permitted in the space being cleared, energies may be transmuted through use of a palm-sized quartz crystal instead of a smudge stick. To "program" a crystal, place it in your left hand and declare your intent to transmute all negative energy. As you hold this thought in your mind and heart, its energy will go wherever the crystal is pointed. It helps to have a crystal that can beam a five- or six-foot swath from a distance of ten feet or less. Ask the crystal if it has this capacity, and it will tell you through sensations in your hand, which may soon be warm, tingly, or comfortable.

## Procedure

To clear and cleanse most indoor spaces, only rattling and smudging may be necessary. First, light the smudge stick and then start rattling with one hand while moving the smudge stick so the smoke covers the area before you. The idea is to begin at the front door with the intent of keeping all the energy in front of you, making a clockwise circle throughout the entire building and returning to where you began.

While rattling and smudging, work as intently with the energy as if you were carefully sweeping a room of dust, concentrating on walls, ceiling, floor, crevices, behind doors, and under tables, making sure no area escapes your attention. Rattle out-of-the-way places with extra vigor to remove especially stubborn stale and negative energies that may have lodged there. Sing a power song if you have one; if not, hum or sing whatever sounds of healing and joy you may be given by your guides, spirit helpers, or intuition to help keep you focus enough to dissipate old energy. At times you may feel as if you are in the midst of a whirlwind, with energy activated and transforming all around you. You might also *see* energy breaking up, like glass shattering, or sometimes rising in sludgeline globs.

If distraction occurs, dislodged energy may attach itself to you, in which case it is important to stay grounded, centered, and shielded, and to ask your guides for protection. Overriding feelings of self-doubt, remember that the Creator's love is unconditional and available to help you co-create the best possible outcome for your efforts, including the release of any energy attachment. Then re-establish your focus and pick up the rattling and smudging where you had left off.

When you are finished, thank the Creator for returning all misplaced energy to its destination. Finally, thank the Creator for transmuting the remaining energy into love, light, and creative forces.

## Other Tools—Crystals, Wands, Feathers, and Water

When cleansing spaces, there may be occasions to use other tools, such as crystals, wands, feathers, or water. Different crystals work in distinctive ways to transmute energy. Crystals can be sprinkled in places to raise the vibrational rate of energy or left in stubborn spots for later maintenance from a distance. Laser crystals can be used to amplify the intent of any ceremony and are particularly effective for defining boundaries while clearing land tracts. A laser crystal is a naturally occurring quartz crystal that has grown into a flat, pointed shape capable of directing energy into a tightly focused beam. All crystals have the ability to channel energy projected onto them and to boost energy due to the piezoelectric effect. Because laser crystals amplify intent, their use requires vigilance.

A wand is a tool that both sends and receives energy and also breaks up energy at distances where a rattle cannot reach. It can be a simple object made of bone or wood, or even a twig. Bones or antlers make good wands and have the added advantage of invoking the spirit of the animal to which they belonged—for example, deer spirits generally help and heal, elk spirits have qualities of ruggedness and tenacity, and buffalo spirits have an energy of abundance and self-sufficiency. A wand may also be ornate, with feathers and beads tied to it, and perhaps a crystal inserted into a carved niche at the tip. A very large wand like a staff may be extremely ornate, such as those carried by many shamans, who attach feathers, fur, and sacred objects to them.

A feather makes for a versatile tool since it may be used to direct energy like a wand, waved to break up energy like a rattle, utilized as an antenna to receive guidance, or serve as a conductor to transmit prayers. A feather may be used to clear a space instead of smudging and rattling, although it requires practice to remain focused while doing so.

Water, another tool, is an excellent cleansing agent. For centuries medicine men have cleansed indoor spots by dipping sweetgrass in water and then slinging the water onto them. When using water to cleanse, first consecrate it by holding your open hands over the container while thanking the Creator for blessing the water with healing love and light. Energy from the palm chakras in your hands, combined with the power of prayerful intent, can actually change the molecular structure of the water, making it a more effective agent for cleansing, especially for sprinkling on problem spots. Water, a token of life-giving replenishment, also makes a wonderful offering to the spirits of the land.

## Sound Vibration

Raising its vibrational level through sound increases the positive energy of a place. The vibration caused by rattling breaks up energy, but sound vibration is powerful in other ways as well. For instance, playing sacred music of a high vibrational level will suffuse a place with positive energy. The chants of Tibetan monks, for example, have low tones that nonetheless exude an extremely high vibrational level.[3]

Drumming is another excellent way to raise the vibrational level of a space. It can transmute energies, increase the ability to perceive non-ordinary reality, and effect cures over vast distances.[4] In the absence of a drum, a person could sing and chant to connect with and transmute energy. Chanting can include religious mantras, sacred sayings, prayers or other verses that have sacred meaning to the individual.

The most powerful means of using voice to activate energy is through a power song, or heart song, that expresses the person's unique positive energies, traits, and intents. Native peoples have used this form of sound vibration for millennia, usually discovering their power songs through fasting and prayer. If you have found your power song, use it to suffuse a place with the energies in you that are being guided to do this work. If you have not yet discovered your power song, consider singing hymns instead, or prayer songs, or joyful melodies from your heart that arise naturally in doing this work.

## Large Buildings

While rattling and smudging are sufficient to effectively clear the energies present in most apartments, homes, and businesses, large buildings require something more. The following procedure will first activate or accelerate the building's MerKaBa, and then connect it to the Christ Consciousness Grid. The purpose of connecting the building's light body to the energy layer above the earth is twofold: to assist humanity through the present shift of the ages and to help accelerate this shift in accordance with the differential equations of Edward Lorenz, originator of the now famous "butterfly effect."

The procedure begins with the recognition that every structure has a power spot from which energy emanates, often considered the "heart" of the space. It is also important to understand that every structure has a light body composed of counter-rotating spirals of energy that, when spinning quickly in a certain ratio, automatically repel most negative energy but when spinning slowly, attract stagnant energy and low-level entities.[5] To get this energy rotating at optimum speed, you would operate from the building's power spot, just as you operate from your heart to effect changes in your body.

## Procedure

To cleanse a large structure, first find the power spot using sensation and intuition. When standing in a power spot, it will simply feel right. You may hear a buzz or hum, experience increased energy in your heart or the pit of your stomach, feel as if your feet are suddenly rooted in place, or have the sensation of walking downhill. If the power spot is embedded in a wall or object, you may notice a subtle wind flowing from the area or experience a sensation similar to walking into a cold building and feeling a sudden flush of warmth from a radiant heater.

After you have discovered the power spot, sit on or near it cross-legged and take a moment to ground and center yourself. Then pray for your guides, angels, and power animals to accelerate the energy of the building to maximum speed. Use whatever method is necessary to reach the Stillpoint—drumming, employing a breathing technique, meditating, singing, chanting, or listening to music. To do this by breathing, inhale slowly from the pelvis and allow the lungs to expand, feeling the energy of the place ground, center, and heal you. Hold your breath for a few seconds, then slowly exhale, emptying the lungs and mind completely. When you feel the MerKaBa energy starting to speed up, disengage; also be ready to disengage anytime you feel your own energy getting sapped. The goal is to give 10 percent of your personal energy and let your guides, angels, and power animals do the rest. Compared with land areas, connecting manmade structures to the Christ Consciousness Grid generally requires more personal energy.

Once the building's light body is functioning under the power of its own life force, ask your guides and angels to "write the connection" between the structure being cleared and the Christ Consciousness Grid. Next, imagine the energies of the power spot establishing a link with the grid and subsequently undergoing transmutation.

## Stubborn Spots

When clearing structures, particular spots may pose difficulties, requiring additional techniques as well as persistence. If energy is trapped in walls or objects, toss a couple of small crystals into the space and come back to it later, realizing that it will need more attention. From time to time, revisit this spot and drum, rattle, or play sacred music until eventually higher energy vibrations dislodge or transmute the energies.

Another problem arises when an underground stream below a house causes energies in the surrounding areas to drift under the house and become stuck. Once you intuit that such a situation exists, consider breaking up the energy with sound vibration and refreshing the area regularly to keep energy from getting stuck there. Use a high-frequency vibration, such as sacred music, to break up the blocked energy so that it flows freely. For instance, you could place a portable CD player or sound-system speaker near the area and play sacred music. It doesn't have to be loud; the frequency is what's needed to keep the area clear or at least routinely cleansed. Alternatively, a laser crystal or wand can be used to dissipate stuck energy and create flow. The same techniques can prove beneficial in portions of large buildings used to store energy that has been brought in from the outside, such as toxic waste areas and blood banks.

If a place has a great deal of locked energy—due, for example, to violence or other negative activity—the following ritual can help dispel it. Fashion two prayer sticks from branches of a tree, or carved pieces of wood, each at least a foot long. Pray over the sticks while wrapping yarn, ribbon, or cloth strips around each of them, allowing the ends to hang free. Ask the Creator to use these sticks for healing.

Then sprinkle cornmeal or tobacco on the surrounding property, making a circle that is large enough to sit in. Place the firmly wound stick on the ground, asking the Creator to draw all the negative energy into that stick. Plant the other stick in the ground near the edge of the circle, letting the yarn, ribbon, or cloth strips blow freely in the breeze. Next, pick up the first stick and break it in two, placing the pieces in the center of the circle. Ask the Creator to break the attachment of negativity to this place and to let the wind transmute the negativity into healing love and light.

This is an ancient rite performed with variations in different cultures. It always involves two features: one stick is consecrated to hold negative energy then broken so that energy is released, and the wind as a physical manifestation of the Creator's will is used to transmute the energy.

## Maintenance

Once a building's light body is connected to the Christ Consciousness Grid, there's very little that needs to be done except to ensure periodically that the light body is spinning as it should, which you can do by leaving a few small crystals here and there within the structure. Since crystals channel whatever energy is projected onto them, you can perform maintenance from afar by visioning the crystals left behind then projecting onto them an intent to boost the energy of a given place in the building with the energy provided by your guides, angels, and the Creator.

## *Outdoor Spaces*

### Small Land Areas

The procedure for clearing small land areas of two acres or less is much the same as for clearing a structure, except that the area's boundary must be created since there are no walls. To create a boundary for a small land area, draw a perimeter with your mind's eye as you walk the land, imagining it as sacred space. Walk clockwise to contain energy, and counterclockwise to break up or expand energy. While doing this, you can rattle if it feels right, use a feather as a wand to define the boundary, or sprinkle pinches of tobacco to circumscribe the space. In addition, you can sing a song from the heart as an expression of gratitude to the Creator, the purpose of which is to utter sacred sounds to identify with the Creator and function as a co-creator in making the space sacred. To this end, ask that the space be protected from all harm and that all beings within it be blessed and viewed as sacred.

When clearing land, the boundary should be permeable to allow blessings to flow in and out like the breath. However, when protection is desired a laser crystal may be used to create a tighter boundary that will physically or emotionally repel people. A perimeter of this type set with strong intent becomes a powerful fence, but since it is difficult to maintain it should be undertaken only with good reason.

Once the boundary is set, "read" the features of the land to see what areas need special attention. Rattling, drumming, or praying may be done at these spots to accentuate or disperse energies. Additionally, to draw the attention of local spirits crystals may be placed in these locations, or pieces of cloth that have been consecrated may be tied to prayer sticks and left to flutter in the wind, releasing prayers and functioning as gifts for the spirits of the land. Prayer sticks utilizing the wind reflect the power of *skan,* Lakota for the sacred force of movement, which existed before the Creator and is acknowledged in many cultures, such as Tibet, where it is said to cause prayer flags to manifest prayers.

To connect the circumscribed space to the Christ Consciousness Grid, simply follow the procedure outlined for large buildings. The boundary that has been set defines the light body to be linked with the earth's highest spiritual potential, thereby identifying the specified land as a sacred area for healing, growth, and balance.

## Large Land Areas

To clear large land areas, it helps to meet the spirits of the land first through meditation, drumming, singing, rattling, or dancing. Once a relationship is established, the spirits will be happy to assist. It is possible to clear land from a distance, which may be necessary if it's a large tract, but such an approach would not allow for the joy of communing with the spirits in an intimate manner.

If instead you are clearing a large land area on site, follow the steps for clearing smaller tracts as best you can: set the boundary, bless particular spots, and connect the transmuted energy to the Christ Consciousness Grid. If the area is very large, traverse it in a vehicle, approaching it in a sacred manner from each direction, moving clockwise and stopping at various places to drum, sing a power song, pray, and bless or release whatever types of energy are encountered. Finally, sitting in the power spot, connect the land's light body as defined by the boundary to the Christ Consciousness Grid.

For more refined work, it is also useful to make an energy map of the troublesome places as you intuit them, thus making a record of areas needing further attention. For example, there may be a corner of the land that harbors elementals or contains portals into other dimensions. In such instances, you would ask your guides for advice on how to proceed.

After all this has been done, drop or slightly bury crystals at spots that "feel right" for purposes of future maintenance, when you may want to connect with the land from a distance. Since you have given energy to the land and received energy from it, your connection with the land is likely to endure. And just as you helped raise the vibrational level of the land, so can the land function as an energy bank from which you may draw when necessary in the future.

Despite having to mark boundaries, it is generally easier to work with land than with structures because man-made structures have a coherent pattern of energy set by intent that actually resists other forms of energy, while land is a storehouse of incredible power with the entire earth's force behind it. And since the Christ Consciousness Grid is already part of the earth's holistic system, connecting a piece of the earth with itself is not difficult, requiring only intent.

## Items Needed to Clear and Cleanse Outdoor Spaces

*Rattle, crystals, or wand.* Utilized to set intent for creating a boundary.

*Tobacco or cornmeal (optional).* Used to mark a boundary and sanctify a space.

*Small crystals (optional).* Scattered to focus energy.

*Drum (optional).* Used to intensify a vibration, particularly while connecting a place to the Christ Consciousness Grid.

## Procedure

*Meet the spirits of the land.* Every tract of land is inhabited by spirits. Open your heart to greet them and request their help.

*Draw a boundary.* Walk the land in a circular way, from east to south to west, back to east, to create a boundary and observe features. The boundary may be set using tobacco or cornmeal, or merely intent reinforced with a wand, rattle, or crystal.

*Sing your power song.* If you have a power song, sing it while working; if not, give voice to whatever "comes up" as a sound of healing and joy. Continue singing and walking the land until you return to where you began.

*Sit in the power spot.* Here, where all the energies of the circumscribed land are focused, you can connect it to the Christ Consciousness Grid by raising its vibrational rate through drumming or intent.

## Liberating Slumbering Earth Energies

After clearing procedures, the land should be resonating at a high vibrational rate. This will not only cause flowers, crops, and wildlife to flourish more abundantly, it may also awaken slumbering earth energies that have been inactive for some time.

Merely acknowledging the potential for the manifestation of miracles increases the possibility of their appearance. The earth and her spirits have an energy and a powerful process of their own that can be activated by the force of human intent. Awaken ourselves and we animate all that is around us—the birds, the animals, the trees, and the earth spirits—thereby creating the potential for increased blessings and elevated energies.

We are all connected in an interwoven web of life, and when we awaken the divinity of the land, we release energy that benefits the world. This occurs because our world is a hologram—meaning that each point of the whole is the whole in microcosm. When we do work on one place, we are really doing work on all places. Likewise, when in spirit we go beyond reflecting the highest energies of the universe, we are the universe, speaking to the universe.

Consequently, when we awaken slumbering energies of the land, we awaken our own highest potential, and the highest potential that naturally exists on the earth. As such, we set in motion a cycle of betterment—invigorating energies that will have positive effects again and again into the future, in an increasing spiral of ascension. Ceremonies function in such a manner, causing all life to flourish, particularly when we start small (see Exercise 5) and in a sacred manner (see Exercise 6). Giving our best, we in turn receive the best given by all. This is the way of the heart, the way of life, and the way of the Creator, who gives blessings to us and our world.

### Exercise 5: Start Small and Build Your Way Up

When beginning the practice of clearing buildings or lands, it's best to start small. If you have a modest apartment or yard, perhaps focus on this space at the outset. If you would rather clear a large building or land area, consider first practicing on a small scale, perhaps on a garden.

Follow the directions in this chapter by delineating the spot with a boundary, asking for guidance, finding the Stillpoint, grounding, centering, and shielding. Then offer prayers and proceed to rattle and smudge while circling the space clockwise. Be aware, especially in places with many flowers and trees, that elementals are likely to be present, embracing the energy and enhancing it. When finished, close the ceremony by giving thanks.

You may soon notice that the place has a new vibrancy: the colors of the flowers and trees will seem brighter, the air cleaner, and plants healthier. To maintain the higher energy vibration, go back to the spot from time to time and repeat the ceremony.

## Exercise 6: Gathering Ceremonial Objects in a Sacred Manner

Learning to gather ceremonial objects in a sacred matter is an important aspect of successfully performing release ceremonies. Plants, crystals, and other objects used for energy work should be approached respectfully and their help in ceremonies requested. For example, when gathering a plant such as sage or cedar, first ask the plant if you may use it for clearing or cleansing. Then listen for a response, usually experienced as a feeling of yes or no. If you determine that permission has been granted, take a small amount of the plant and leave something in return—perhaps a pinch of tobacco or corn. This shows respect, giving something of value for the value taken.

If a large amount of plant material is required, do not harm one plant by taking too much but instead take a little from it and then ask if there is another plant that would like to contribute to a positive activity for the benefit of all. One or more plants may answer affirmatively if asked with sincerity and respect. This manner of asking for help also extends to crystals and other objects used for energy work. In cultivating an understanding that all beings are connected, we strive to live in balance and harmony, each offering gifts and each respected for its uniqueness.

When selecting any ceremonial object for purchase, such as a smudge stick, rattle, drum, wand, feather, or crystal, ensure that its energy is positive. Holding it in your hand, close your eyes, and see what arises. If it evokes good feelings, perhaps even a vision of how it should be used, the chances are its energy is positive. If it feels dead and lifeless, cold to the touch, or heavy, look elsewhere for such an object. Although it is often possible to raise the vibrational rate of an object, rarely is it worth the time and effort.

# From the Energy Notebook: A Complex Cleansing

Most places require only one sweep, or tour around the area, for cleansing, but some need more complex energy work, such as dealing with stubborn energy spots, portals, or entities. For example, I was once asked to cleanse a building over one hundred years old, next to the historic site of a tragedy in which scores of people had died. The building covered an entire city block and had four stories filled with shops of various kinds, including some selling antiques, books, and clothing.

The owners knew there were spirits in the place, having heard "bumps in the night," which didn't concern them, but they wanted more business and therefore a more generally positive energy, and no refurbishing they had done so far had helped. The building looked normal on the outside; only after I went into the Stillpoint, asked my guides and angels to help me, and began to rattle and smudge throughout the building, did the trouble became apparent. The problem wasn't just stagnant energy or a sluggish MerKaBa, but the whole gamut: embedded stale energy, spirit fragments, trapped spirits, all manner of other entities, and portals. This was clearly not going to be a "one sweep" operation.

On the first sweep, I cleared the place by rattling and smudging and tossed small crystals into the trouble spots of embedded energy with the intention of returning. Along the way, I discovered several lost souls and spirit fragments. The trapped souls appeared either like bodies asleep on the floor or standing dazed, while the spirit fragments looked like fleeting shadows. Two entities I couldn't identify, other than their size and aura of power, were guarding a portal and watching me in a state of detachment. The portal appeared as a vortex of energy on the top floor of the building, where the owners were designing a museum to house relics from the tragedy that had occurred next door.

When I'm clearing a place, rattling and smudging put me in a quasi-shamanic state, enabling me to "walk between the worlds" and see entities of different dimensions superimposed over ordinary, 3-D material reality. My primary means of reception is visual, but sometimes I hear or feel things instead. If entities are present where you are working and you have not yet developed second sight, you can still sense them—often by feeling something "brush by," noticing a chill in a room, thinking you are being watched, or having objects appear and disappear or be moved as if by an external force.

On the second sweep, I went back to the areas where there were trapped souls and drummed for them, conducting a psychopomp to urge them toward the light. Some didn't want to go, so I merely acknowledged them because the building's owners had said that if I found any harmless spirits they didn't especially want them to leave.

Next, I engaged the two guardians of the portal in conversation to determine their function. They appeared as tall, extraterrestrial or inter-dimensional beings made of energy rings, one atop the other. I didn't have to speak, for they read my thoughts projected to them.

I asked silently, "Why are you here?" They answered that they were observing.

I asked if the portal was theirs. They looked puzzled then replied that the portal simply "was" and that they had been guarding it so that no negative entities would enter, allowing passage only to those who had died there and retained a connection to the place. My sense was that some spirits of the land were using the portal to travel inter-dimensionally.

I asked my power animal if these entities were OK or if they should be removed, only to learn that they were doing no harm. (Had they been doing harm, I would have immediately asked my power animal to remove them and seal the portal.) The guardians seemed to hear and understand this conversation, so I asked them if they would continue to stand guard and keep negative energies from entering the portal. They said they would, and my power animal agreed they had sufficient power for the task, so I left the two guardians alone.

Following this, I accelerated the building's MerKaBa and connected it to the Christ Consciousness Grid. This was accomplished through drumming from the building's power spot, which after great effort I determined was in a closet on the third floor. The owners, delighted with this finding, said they had long known "there was something spooky up there," and the newly discovered "tenants" made interesting lore to share with customers in connection with the historic site next door, adding mystique to the place. After the cleansing ritual, the stores did a booming business.

## Review

How to perform release ceremonies:
- Ask permission of the spirits of the place and give a prayer for guidance.
- Find the Stillpoint; ground, center, and shield.
- Mark the boundaries of the place and stay present while rattling and smudging.
- Give thanks when finished, closing the ceremony.

# Final Thoughts

In undertaking energy work for structures or land, it is helpful to maintain a broad perspective on goals. As well as transmuting negative to positive energy for purposes of increased personal health, happiness and earth balance, you are contributing to elevating energy forces for humanity in general. At the same time, it is best to keep the limitations of such energy work in mind. Sometimes, despite your best efforts to transmute negative to positive energy, the power of karma and free will cannot be mitigated. Specifically, others can destroy your work if this is their focused intention from the present or a previous lifetime. Additionally, divine beings may intercede to alter an outcome or provide necessary teachings. Nonetheless, through focused energy work it is possible to optimize the positive energy available and, along with natural forces, keep buildings and lands free of negative energy.

Places that have undergone considerable energy work shine brightly, appearing in non-ordinary reality like searchlights cutting swaths of light into the firmament. Such places repel negative energy and attract positive energy, making them healthy environments for humanity.

Finally, all the procedures and ideas discussed in this book reflect love and gratitude that we share this planet with such a diversity of life. In doing energy work, always keep in mind that, according to the Creator's plan, all land and all beings are sacred. Our greatest accomplishments result not from mighty acts of strength but from co-creatively honoring the energies of the earth and trusting the whisperings of our guides and angels. Though we are small compared to an earthquake, the "still small voice" is greater than all others.

When conscious of our power as co-creators guided by Spirit, we are capable of unimaginable feats. Among them, we become what we see and what we see becomes as we would have it be. As a result, everything we perceive—every rock, tree, plant, animal, ally, and spirit of the land—becomes empowered, generating a sacred circle that in turn enlivens us. That is the secret of environmental shamanism: in healing our natural surroundings, we heal ourselves.

# Other Resources

Long-distance Reiki work is a powerful modality that I often use, but since it requires extensive study, training, and initiation into the Reiki tradition, I have not outlined the procedures in this book. However, I encourage individuals to explore Reiki. William Lee Rand, founder of the International Center for Reiki Training, teaches a method of healing land which employs Reiki symbols. Through the ICRT, Reiki practitioners have helped to heal trouble spots around the world.

For more information, contact:

The International Center for Reiki Training,
21421 Hilltop Street, Unit #28,
Southfield, MI 48034.
Phone: 800-332-8112.
Web site: http://www.reiki.org

Another valuable resource for healing lands and waters are the classes offered by Sandra Ingerman based on her book *Medicine for the Earth: How to Transform Personal and Environmental Toxins*. You may write to Ms. Ingerman to obtain a schedule of her Medicine for the Earth workshops, at:

P.O. Box 4757, Santa Fe,
NM 87502.
Web site: http://www.shamanicvisions.com

# Notes

## Chapter 1

1. This technique, called the Gassho Meditation, is taught by William Lee Rand of the International Center for Reiki Training.

## Chapter 2

1. For more information on the military's experiments in the paranormal, see Bob Frisell's *Something in This Book Is True* (Berkeley, Calif.: Frog Ltd., 1997) and Drunvalo Melchizedek's *Ancient Secrets of the Flower of Life*, vols. 1 and 2 (Flagstaff, Ariz.: Light Technology Publishing, 1990).

2. For more information on psychopomp and training in shamanism, as well as a state-by-state directory of local shamanic practitioners, contact the Foundation for Shamanic Studies, P.O. Box 1939, Mill Valley, CA 94942. Phone: 415-380-8282. Web site: http://www.shamanism.org

3. See resources for information on psychopomp in Note 2, for example.

4. Carlos Castaneda, *Journey To Ixtlan: The Lessons of Don Juan* (New York: Simon & Schuster, 1977).

## Chapter 3

1. The Foundation for Shamanic Studies, in its Basic Shamanism class, teaches how to find one's power animal. The foundation is a nonprofit international educational organization dedicated to the preservation and teaching of shamanic knowledge for the welfare of the planet and its inhabitants. It is a 501(c)(3) public charitable organization; contributions are tax deductible as allowed by law.

Scholarship rebates are available to Native Americans on tribal rolls for all FSS workshops. See Chapter 2, Note 2, for address and Web site. If in addition you wish to study with a teacher, contact Omega at http://www.omega.org or Alberto Villoldo's Four Winds Society at http://www.thefourwinds.org

2. A problem with preserving sacred lands is that currently there is no way to assure the protection of a sacred site and no cause of action. Consequently, there is no general compendium of sacred lands, although local tribes and organizations assume responsibility for protecting specific sites. In 2001, meetings with tribal leaders and experts from around the country were held in Denver and Boulder, Colorado, called The Native American Sacred Lands Forum, in which preservation of sacred spaces was discussed. Participants concluded, among other things, that the primary applicable federal laws, the American Indian Religious Freedom Act of 1978 (AIRFA) and the National Historic Preservation Act and Executive Order 13007, were inadequate for protecting sacred spaces; state and county laws were virtually nonexistent; and federal agencies in charge of administering federal lands, such as the Department of the Interior and the National Park Service, were often either hostile or indifferent to allowing access to sacred sites for the performance of sacred ceremonies, even when provided for by law. Recommendations included the establishment of a sacred lands protection coalition of tribes, non-recognized nations, churches, environmental groups, and others; the compilation of a complete list of preservation offices and contacts, along with applicable county and state laws; and useful national legislation. The forum further recommended the formulation of a definition of sacred site that includes "newly created sacred sites," power places, and sites for fasting and vision quests. An additional recommendation was that religious practitioners using sacred sites on federal lands be

exempted from access fees and that access hours be extended to ensure that three- or four-day fasts (vision quests) and sunup-to-sundown ceremonies could be held.

AIRFA was originally intended to safeguard all Native American spiritual practices, but the law failed to protect sacred sites in subsequent court tests. The Native American Free Exercise of Religion Act, introduced in Congress in 1993, included provisions for sacred site protection; however, this act was dropped with only a small section included in AIRFA in 1994. In 2002, a Sacred Lands Protection Coalition was formed through the National Congress of American Indians, Association on American Indian Affairs, Seventh Generation Fund, and the Native American Rights Fund. In 2002 and again in 2003, a Native American Sacred Lands Act was introduced, but no law has resulted.

Given the inconsistencies in laws and regulations regarding sacred sites, both in local jurisdictions and among federally protected lands, it's no surprise that compiling a list of sacred sites and organizations would be difficult. Publicizing such a list could also jeopardize them.

Until a judicial and legislative framework is in place to protect sacred sites, it is probably best to keep them covert or rely on public pressure for open access. To avoid discrimination on the basis of race or religion, any federal or state legislation regarding public lands, while ensuring Native American access, should also not require tribal affiliation or blood quanta imperatives. It should be enough simply to affirm that an individual's religion includes honoring the land and its spirits.

3. See historian Robert S. McElvaine's seminal work, *Eve's Seed: Biology, the Sexes, and the Course of History* (New York: McGraw-Hill, 2001).

4. The Manataka American Indian Council (MAIC), a nonprofit, tax-exempt 501(c)(3) organization, can be contacted at P.O. Box 476, Hot Springs Reservation, AR

71902-0476; phone: 501-627-0555; Web site: www.manataka.org. Only through the sincere dedication and loving care of MAIC—and the unwitting help of the federal government by including the Rainbow Woman's mountain as a park—has the home of this goddess been preserved. MAIC, which also ministers to poor and ill indigenous peoples of all tribes, is a worthy organization for charitable contributions.

## Chapter 4

1. The ability to transmute energy in a substance, particularly water, through intent has been well documented by Japanese researcher Masaru Emoto. See his book *The Message from Water*, vols. 1 and 2 (Tokyo, Japan: Hado Kyoikusha, 2004), or visit his Web site at http://www.masaru-emoto.net

2. The incense I prefer for smudging is Pure Tibetan Herbal Meditation, prepared by Chedora Devi, Swayambhu Temple, Manjushree, Kathmandu, Nepal, and imported by The Himalayan Traders. Another incense that works well for more feminine energies is Kuan Yin Goddess Incense, also made in Nepal and imported by The Himalayan Traders.

3. I use two CDs to clear energy in a room: "Freedom Chants from the Roof of the World" by the Gyuto Monks, RYKODISC 306 Degree Productions, and "Sacred Music, Sacred Dance for Planetary Healing and World Purification" by Tibetan Buddhist monks from the Drepung Loseling Monastery, Music & Arts Programs of America, Inc.

Music with a high vibrational level can actually drive someone from a room when it brings to consciousness suppressed emotions or memories. High-frequency vibration can often expose the "shadow" self—qualities that one doesn't admit to personally and consequently rejects in others. Whether through sounds or other vibration, this is the nature of high-frequency energy work: to bring hidden things to the surface so that they can be recognized and healed.

4.  Native Americans and most other indigenous peoples have known for thousands of years that drumming is a powerful spiritual tool. However, only in recent years has this knowledge been confirmed by science. In the 1960s and 1970s, anthropologist Michael Harner, founder of the Foundation for Shamanic Studies, conducted pioneering work into the effects of drumming which he then outlined in his book *The Way of the Shaman* (New York: Harper, 1980). According to Harner, the drumbeat used to transport native peoples into shamanic states of consciousness closely approximates the base resonant frequency of the earth, which can be measured scientifically. In recent years, Gregg Braden, a geophysicist and author of *Awakening to Zero Point: The Collective Initiation* (Bellevue, Wash.: Radio Bookstore Press, 1997) and *Walking Between the Worlds: The Science of Compassion* (Bellevue, Wash.: Radio Bookstore Press, 1997) continuously measured this frequency and hypothesized that the earth is going through great changes with profound implications for its inhabitants. He concluded that this measurement coincides with the ancient prophecies of the Egyptians, Hopi, Aztecs, and Mayans, as well as those found in the Christian Bible. These prophecies collectively state that the earth will go through transformation and renewal during the "end times," which some say are now beginning.

    The physiological effects of sound, also well documented, include alpha, beta, and theta (psychic) states produced in the brain. See Mitchell L. Gaynor's book *Sounds of Healing: A Physician Reveals the Therapeutic Power of Sound, Voice and Music* (New York: Broadway Books, 1999).

5.  Some of the principles involved are described in Drunvalo Melchizedek's books *Ancient Secrets of the Flower of Life*,

vols. 1 and 2 (Flagstaff, Ariz.: Light Technology Publishing, 1990) and are taught in courses given by Flower of Life Research LLC, P.O. Box 55844, Phoenix, AZ 85078; phone: 602-996-0900; Web site: http://www.floweroflife.org. Although they do not specifically teach land clearing, the books and courses are both highly recommended.

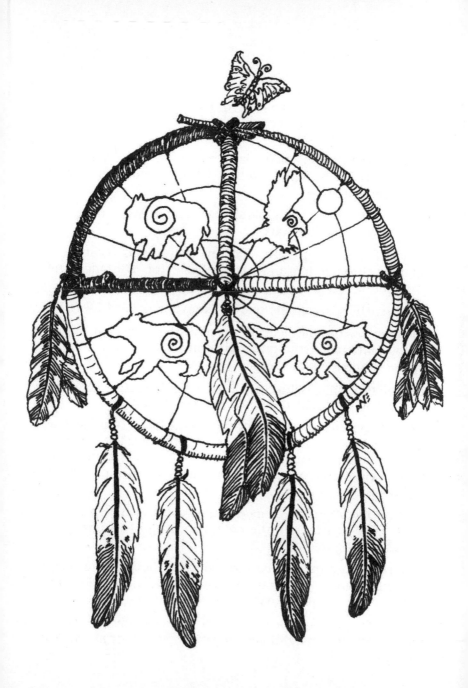

# Glossary

*akashic records.* The energy layer above the earth that holds all records of being, including karmic information and potential realities.

*allies.* Wild spirits of the land that can aid in healing and protecting natural habitats.

*angels.* Emissaries of light of divine origin who accompany humans through life and are available for assistance and inspiration.

*animus.* The spark of life; spark that gives an object life.

*archetypes.* Attributes existing in potential form that can be brought into manifestation; original models after which other similar things are patterned.

*ascension.* Transcending to a higher level of consciousness; the next step in human and planetary evolution.

*aura.* Perceived emanations of the energy body, often seen as colors that show moods, thoughts, or potentials; the energetic fields surrounding the physical body, including physical, etheric, emotional, mental, astral, etheric template, celestial, and causal.

*bodhisattva.* A human being of higher consciousness who has chosen not to ascend to the next plane, in order to bring all beings to enlightenment.

*centering.* Locating the core of consciousness in the body; drawing magnetic energy from the earth and electrical energy from the sun to operate with balanced awareness.

*chakra.* Sanskrit for circle or wheel; the energetic centers in the core of the body, linked together by a central psychic energy channel.

**Christ Consciousness Grid.** An energy layer which surrounds the earth and signifies its highest potential and which was supposedly established by higher beings, often referred to as Ascended Beings, to help humanity through the current "shift of the ages."

**cleansing.** Transmuting energy to a higher, more positive form by raising its vibrational rate.

**clearing.** Dissipating (transmuting) negative energy. Clearing spaces usually also cleanses them since the act of clearing raises the vibrational rate.

**co-creating.** Operating as a partner with the Creator to boost positive energy.

**de-possession.** Removal of entities that have taken possession of a psyche.

**elementals.** Spirits that attend to the earth's energies and manifestations.

**elves.** Spirits of land, forest, and waters.

**energy.** Subtle power manifested through animus, life force, frequency, or cohesion.

**energy body.** A body that exists beyond the physical plane; in humans, such a body extends twenty-seven feet in each direction and thereafter continues into other dimensions. See aura.

**exorcism.** Removal of a foreign entity from the psyche; a ritual of de-possession.

**extraterrestrials.** Beings not of the earth; either visitors from other planets or inter-dimensional travelers.

**fairies.** Spirits of the earth that work with flora and fauna.

**flow of creation.** The divine wind; the movement of energy in a given moment.

**ghosts.** Types of energy fragments that appear to have life but are not usually connected to a living being.

***God vs. Creator.*** God is one, all; Creator is the active aspect of God as expressed in the will of creation.

***goddesses.*** Land spirits of the highest order, usually associated with a place or characteristic; also, humans who have transcended but chosen to remain on earth in spirit form as a means of service.

***grounding.*** Connecting with the earth energetically to ensure that consciousness is not operating from other dimensions or overly affected by other energetic forces.

***guides.*** Spirit helpers, soul brothers or sisters from former or future lifetimes, or spiritual masters who have assumed a supportive role for a particular soul's evolution.

***heart song, or power song.*** A song that expresses the unique, positive energies, traits, and intents of an individual, usually discovered through fasting and prayer.

***higher power.*** God as expressed through one's highest nature.

***Ix Chel.*** Mayan goddess known for nurturing and protection, especially of women and children.

***Jung, Carl G.*** Swiss psychiatrist (1875-1961) who explored aspects of the human psyche and wrote about such notions as the collective unconscious, archetypes, and synchronicity.

***kachinas.*** Supernatural beings revered by the Hopi and appearing as messengers from the spirit world.

***karma.*** Continuation of cause and effect across lifetimes either through actions and choices made in this and previous lifetimes or through pre-birth choices in the spirit state for the experiences and lessons of this lifetime.

***laser crystal.*** A crystal, usually flat and thin, effective in projecting energy over long distances and creating boundaries.

***ley lines.*** Grids that crisscross the earth and hold potential electromagnetic energy, many of which were identified by ancient peoples, who built sacred sites over them.

**life-force energy.** Energy that is all around us, from water or wind moving; energy that is emitted by the earth.

**light body.** Energetic body; a term often used to express the quality of energy around a person, as opposed to their physical body. See MerKaBa.

**matter.** Patterns of energy we perceive as having substance.

**medicine wheel.** A Native American system of prayer, meditation, and discovery, recognizing that life follows a circle. The wheel's directions, from which all things are said to derive, comprise East (newness, discovery), South (youth, growth, healing), West (introspection, setting sun, light within), North (wisdom, elders, ancestors, those who have gone before), Center (soul, spirit), Above (Heavenly Father), and Below (Earthly Mother).

**meridians.** Lines along the body where energy is channeled; often used in acupuncture and other energy medicine to effect healing.

**MerKaBa.** In sacred geometry, a star tetrahedron; an energetic framework that forms a blueprint for spirit to attach to and from which, in plants and animals, DNA creates a physical expression; a geometric form that includes the light body; a pattern of energy shared by animals, plants, stones, and all objects, including those that are man-made.

**mind of God.** Expansion of human thought to higher consciousness as far as is conceivable.

**morphogenic field.** A universal field encoding the basic pattern of an object. From the Greek morphe, which means form, and genesis, which denotes coming into being. Non-corporeal beings manifest in 3-D reality through morphogenic resonance.

**native peoples.** Indigenous cultures practicing traditional earth- and nature-based ways.

**non-ordinary reality.** Reality as seen when everyday constraints and predispositions are eliminated through trance or other methods.

*piezoelectric effect.* An inherent mechanical trait of crystals that boosts electrical. energy.

*portal.* A vortex through which objects and entities can pass from one dimension of reality to another while realm shifting.

*power animal.* An animal that offers guidance and protection; a totem.

*power song, or heart song.* A song that expresses the unique, positive energies, traits, and intents of an individual, usually discovered through fasting and prayer.

*power spot.* A place where all energies of a structure or tract of land are focused.

*prana.* Universal life-force energy.

*prayer stick.* A stick, either ornate or plain, that has been consecrated through prayer, wrapped with cloth, ribbon, or yarn, and most often planted in the ground to carry a prayer.

*psychopomp.* A ritual to help guide a trapped soul to the afterlife.

*Quan Yin.* Asian goddess; spirit of compassion.

*rattling.* Shaking a rattle to break up energy.

*realm shifting.* The movement of objects between dimensions; while some objects, such as quartz crystals, do this routinely because of their energetic composition, others will disappear and reappear only when near a portal.

*Reiki.* A Japanese form of energy medicine involving sacred symbols and guides; use of the hands to channel healing energy.

*sacred circle.* All beings in our lives-past, present, and future-who are connected to us.

*shaman.* Siberian term meaning "one who sees in the dark"; a person who uses earth energy, guides, and power animals for insight; a medicine man or woman.

**shielding.** Creating, through intent, a protective energy layer around you to deflect external negative energy.

**shift of the ages.** Powerful changes in energy patterns now occurring on earth as a prelude to earth transformations and humanity's eventual development of higher consciousness.

**skan.** From the Lakota, meaning power of the wind; a sacred force of movement; that which existed before God; life-force energy; the principle that manifests prayers from prayer flags.

**smudging.** Burning a plant such as sage, cedar, or sweetgrass to purify the energy of an area.

**soul.** The essential life force, or essence, of a being that is eternal from lifetime to lifetime.

**space.** Any defined area, including the objects within it.

**spiral of ascension.** Spiral of life that offers a changing perspective as new lessons are encountered and old ones repeated, until the lessons are finally learned.

**spirit.** The essential quality of a being as an expression of soul; aligned with soul purpose.

**spirit quest.** Following only what spirit dictates, usually over a course of days.

**sprite.** A land spirit usually residing in a particular place.

**star beings.** Beings from the stars whom cultures around the globe and throughout time have claimed influenced human development; some sacred spots are devoted to honoring them.

**Stillpoint.** An inner place of total silence and stillness, where intuition and creativity originate and balance can be found; the source of being.

**thought forms.** Organized patterns of energy, either free floating or embedded in a space, that can be broken up by rattling or other means of transmutation.

**transmutation.** Changing energy from one state to another, such as changing water to ice or vapor, and vice versa; changing negative, or inert, energy into positive, or active, energy, or neutralizing energy to be reabsorbed by the earth. Ancient practices involved burying an energized object in the ground, burning it with fire, or submerging it in water.

**vibrational rate / vibrational frequency.** The measurable level of energy exhibited by a person, place, or object; the higher the rate, the closer to the source, or optimal, healthful wholeness.

**vortices.** Doorways or portals into other dimensions; areas where energy in flux can affect time and space.

**wand.** A long, thin implement used to direct energy when pointed. Some are ornate, with carvings, feathers, beads, and similar adornments, while others are as simple as a twig or a feather.

**wild spirit.** A spirit of the land that usually inhabits wilderness areas away from civilization or contact with humans; allies.

**will of creation.** Energy of the moment moving from one state to another; the potential to transform to another manifestation.

# Bibliography

Alvord, Lori Arviso, M.D., *The Scalpel and the Silver Bear*. New York: Bantam, 1999.

Andrews, Ted. *Animal-Speak: The Spiritual and Magical Powers of Creatures Great and Small*. St. Paul, Minn: Llewellyn Publications, 1998.

——. *Enchantment of the Faerie Realm: Communicate with Nature Spirits & Elementals*. St. Paul, Minn: Llewellyn Publications, 1998.

Bear Heart, with Molly Larkin. *The Wind Is My Mother: The Life and Teachings of a Native American Shaman*. New York: Berkeley Books, 1996.

Bentov, Itzhak. *Stalking the Wild Pendulum: On the Mechanics of Consciousness*. Rochester, Vt.: Destiny Books, 1988.

Black Elk, Wallace H., et al. *Black Elk: The Sacred Ways of a Lakota Medicine Man*. San Francisco: Harper, 1991.

Boissiere, Robert. *Meditations with the Hopi*. Santa Fe, N.M.: Bear and Company, 1986.

Boyd, Doug. *Mad Bear: Spirit, Healing, and the Sacred in the Life of a Native American Medicine Man*. New York: Touchstone, 1994.

——. *Rolling Thunder*. New York: Dell, 1974.

Braden, Gregg. *The Isaiah Effect*. New York: Harmony Books, 2000.

————. *Awakening to Zero Point: The Collective Initiation.* Bellevue, Wash.: Radio Bookstore Press, 1997.

————. *Walking Between the Worlds: The Science of Compassion.* Bellevue, Wash.: Radio Bookstore Press, 1997.

Brueyere, Rosalyn L. *Wheels of Light: Chakras, Auras, and the Healing Energy of the Body.* New York: Simon & Schuster, 1989.

Buhner, Stephen Harrod. *Sacred Plant Medicine: Explorations in the Practice of Indigenous Herbalism.* Coeur d'Alene, Idaho: Raven Press, 1996.

Capra, Fritjof. *The Tao of Physics.* Berkeley, Calif.: Shambala, 1975.

Carroll, Lee. *The Journey Home: A Kryon Parable.* Carlsbad, Calif.: Light Technology Publishing, 1997.

Carroll, Lee, and Jan Tober. *The Indigo Children: The New Kids Have Arrived.* Carlsbad, Calif.: Hay House, 1999.

Castaneda, Carlos. *Journey To Ixtlan: The Lessons of Don Juan.* New York: Simon & Schuster, 1977.

————. *The Teachings of Don Juan: A Yaqui Way of Knowledge.* New York: Ballantine, 1969.

Catches, Pete S., Sr., Peter V. Catches, ed. *Sacred Fireplace (Oceti Wakan): Life and Teachings of a Lakota Medicine Man.* Santa Fe, N.M.: Clear Light Publishers, 1999.

Eagle Feather, Ken. *A Toltec Path.* Charlottesville, Va.: Hampton Roads, 1995.

Eaton, Evelyn, and Narca Shorr (illus.). *I Send a Voice.* New York: Quest Books, 1978.

Emoto, Masaru. *The Message from Water.* vols. 1 and 2. Tokyo, Japan: Hado Kyoikusha, 2004.

Frissell, Bob. *Something In This Book Is True.* Berkeley, Calif.: Frog Ltd., 1997.

Gaynor, Mitchell L., M.D. *Sounds of Healing: A Physician Reveals the Therapeutic Power of Sound, Voice and Music.* New York: Broadway Books, 1999.

Gerber, Richard, M.D. *Vibrational Medicine: New Choices for Healing Ourselves.* Santa Fe, N.M.: Bear and Company, 1996.

Gillentine, Julie. *Tarot and Dream Interpretation.* St. Paul, Minn.: Llewellyn Publications, 2003.

Harner, Michael. *The Way of the Shaman.* New York: Harper, 1980.

Hunt, Valerie V. *Infinite Mind: Science of the Human Vibrations of Consciousness.* Malibu, Calif.: Malibu Publishing Co., 1989.

Ingerman, Sandra. *Shamanic Journeying: A Beginner's Guide.* Boulder, Colo.: Sounds True, 2004.

——. *Medicine for the Earth: How to Transform Personal and Environmental Toxins.* New York: Three Rivers Press, 2000.

——. *Welcome Home: Following Your Soul's Journey Home.* San Francisco: Harper, 1993.

——. *Soul Retrieval: Mending the Fragmented Self.* San Francisco: Harper, 1991.

Jacoby, Kathleen. *The Vision of the Grail.* San Francisco: Lightlines Publishing Co., 2001.

Lame Deer, John, Archie Fire, and Richard Erdoes. *Gift of Power: The Life and Teachings of a Lakota Medicine Man*. Santa Fe, N.M.: Bear and Company, 1994.

Lame Deer, John, and Richard Erdoes. *Lame Deer, Seeker of Visions*. New York: Simon & Schuster, 1994.

Leary, Timothy. *Change Your Brain*. Berkeley: Ronin Publishing, 2000.

Lungold, Ian. *Mayan Calendar and Conversion Codex*. Sedona, Ariz.: Majix Inc., 1999.

MacEowen, Frank. *The Spiral of Memory and Belonging: A Celtic Path of Soul and Kinship*. Novato, Calif.: New World Library, 2004.

Mails, Thomas E. *Fools Crow*. Lincoln, Nebr.: University of Nebraska Press, 1990.

McElvaine, Robert S. *Eve's Seed: Biology, the Sexes, and the Course of History*. New York: McGraw-Hill, 2001.

Medicine Eagle, Brooke. *The Last Ghost Dance: A Guide for Earth Mages*. New York: Wellspring/Ballantine, 2000.

———. *Buffalo Woman Comes Singing*. New York: Ballantine Books, 1991.

Melchizedek, Drunvalo. *Ancient Secrets of the Flower of Life*. vols. 1 and 2. Flagstaff, Ariz.: Light Technology Publishing, 1990.

Mehl-Madrona, Lewis, M.D. *Coyote Medicine*. New York: Simon & Schuster, 1997.

Morgan, Marlo. *Mutant Message Down Under*. New York: Harper Perennial, 1995.

# Bibliography

Naparstek, Belleruth. *Your Sixth Sense: Unlocking the Power of Your Intuition*. New York: Harper, 1997.

Pert, Candace B., Ph.D. *Molecules of Emotion: The Science Behind Mind-Body Medicine*. New York: Simon & Schuster, 1999.

Rae, Allison Bluestar. *Stars & Myths: A Path to Higher Consciousness*. Paonia, Colo.: Earth Star Publications, 2002.

Rand, William Lee. *Reiki for a New Millennium*. Southfield, Mich.: Vision Publications, 1998.

———. *Reiki: The Healing Touch: First and Second Degree Manual*. Southfield, Mich.: Vision Publications, 1991.

Redfield, James. *The Celestine Vision*. New York: Warner Books, 1997.

Rinpoche, Sogyal. *The Tibetan Book of Living and Dying*. New York: Harper, 1994.

Ruiz, Don Miguel. *The Four Agreements*. San Rafael, Calif.: Amber-Allen Publishing, 1997.

Sambhava, Padma, and Robert A. Thurman (trans). *The Tibetan Book of the Dead*. New York: Bantam, 1994.

Sams, Jamie. *Dancing the Dream: The Seven Sacred Paths of Human Transformation*. New York: HarperCollins, 1998.

Stein, Diane. *Essential Reiki: A Complete Guide to an Ancient Healing Art*. Freedom, Calif.: The Crossing Press, 1995.

Storm, Hyemeyohsts. *Seven Arrows*. New York: Ballantine Books, 1985.

Tolle, Eckhart. *Stillness Speaks*. Novato, Calif.: New World Library, 2003.

———. *The Power of Now: A Guide to Spiritual Enlightenment.* Novato, Calif.: New World Library, 1999.

Virtue, Doreen. *Divine Prescriptions: Using Your Sixth Sense— Spiritual Solutions for You and Your Loved Ones.* Los Angeles: Renaissance Books, 2000.

Weiss, Brian, M.D. *Messages from the Masters.* New York: Warner Books, 2000.

———. *Many Lives, Many Masters,* New York: Fireside, 1988.

Windrider, Kiara. *Doorway to Eternity: A Guide to Planetary Ascension.* Mt. Shasta, Calif.: Heaven on Earth Project, 2002.

Zukov, Gary. *The Dancing Wu Li Masters: An Overview of the New Physics.* New York: William Morrow, 1979.

FINDHORN PRESS

*Life-Changing Books*

Consult our catalogue online
(with secure order facility) on
*www.findhornpress.com*


For information on the Findhorn Foundation:
*www.findhorn.org*